A. G. Spalding

Spalding's base ball guide

and official league book for ... : a complete hand book of the national game of

base ball ..

A. G. Spalding

Spalding's base ball guide
 and official league book for ... : a complete hand book of the national game of base ball ..

ISBN/EAN: 9783741174759

Manufactured in Europe, USA, Canada, Australia, Japa

Cover: Foto ©Andreas Hilbeck / pixelio.de

Manufactured and distributed by brebook publishing software (www.brebook.com)

A. G. Spalding

Spalding's base ball guide

Experience has shown that in Base Ball and Athle[tic] Goods, as in all other lines of business, unprincipled p[er]sons are always eager to prey on the reputation gained [by] honest dealing and good business management. We reg[ret] to state that we have not escaped the attention of su[ch] parties, who have appropriated our original designs, styl[es] and names, and by using similar illustrations and descriptions, deceive t[he] public into believing that the articles were manufactured by us, and th[at] we are responsible for their inferior quality. A wide acquaintance w[ith] sportsmen and an extended experience with the various sports, has enab[led] us to anticipate the wants of our patrons in securing outfits, and to off[er] only such articles as were perfectly satisfactory for our own use, knowi[ng] by practical tests that they would serve the purpose properly, and [be] unfailing to the purchaser.

In order to protect our customers, and to preserve our reputation, [we] have found it necessary to place our "Trade Mark" on the higher grad[es] of goods that we manufacture and introduce. The care and discriminati[on] exercised in selecting only articles of the highest quality as being wort[hy] of bearing our Trade Mark, has resulted in giving to them a reputation [of] being practically the best of their kind that could be produced.

In our opinion a satisfied customer is the best advertisement that [we] can have, and dealers and individuals will please bear in mind that [in] whatever article our *Trade Mark* appears, we guarantee it to be exact[ly] as represented, and wherever just cause for complaint exists, we w[ill] thank the purchaser for returning the article to us and receiving a perfe[ct] one in return, or the refunding of the purchase money.

Our line of Base Balls is now so well known to the trade, and they a[re] so thoroughly appreciated by the base ball players of the country, that [it] seems almost unnecessary to call special attention to their superior meri[t.] Spalding's League Ball, having stood the severe test of the Nation[al] League for the last nine years, and having again been adopted as the offici[al] ball of that leading organization for 1888, as well as the other promine[nt] professional College and Amateur Associations, gives it a reputation a[nd] sale unequaled by any other ball on the market. *Beware of cheap imit[a]tions;* no League Ball is genuine without our Trade Mark on each box a[nd] ball, and the autograph of

A. G. Spalding

on each label.

We hope that Ball Players will not be misled by the remarks of i[n]terested dealers handling inferior goods, that the articles they offer "a[re] just as good as Spalding's," and at a cheaper price. We accept the[se] frequent references to our goods as the highest compliment that can b[e] paid us, and only ask that purchasers will make their own comparison[s] and be convinced that our goods are really the cheapest, as they certain[ly] are the best. Special trade prices are quoted to dealers on application.

The popular encouragement given to the pursuit of Athletic Sports, recreative Amusements, Gymnastic Exercises, etc., and the comparative scarcity of mediums of instruction on these subjects, suggested the publication of our LIBRARY OF ATHLETIC SPORTS. The benefits of Athletic and other manly exercises, from an educational as well as from a moral and creative point of view, are now so generally recognized that the right method of promoting man's physical welfare should be readily accessible.

		Price each
No. 1.	SPALDING'S OFFICIAL BASE BALL GUIDE	10 Cents
2.	SPALDING'S OFFICIAL LEAGUE BOOK	10 "
3.	SPALDING'S ILLUSTRATED HAND BOOK OF PITCHING AND FIELDING	25 "
4.	SPALDING'S ILLUSTRATED HAND BOOK OF BATTING AND BASE RUNNING	25 "
7.	SPALDING'S ILLUSTRATED FOOT BALL RULES AND REFEREES' BOOK	10 "
8.	SPALDING'S LAWN TENNIS MANUAL	10 "
10.	SPALDING'S OFFICIAL CROQUET MANUAL	10 "
11.	SPALDING'S MANUAL OF BOXING, INDIAN CLUB SWINGING AND MANLY SPORTS	25 "
13.	SPALDING'S HAND BOOK OF SPORTING RULES AND TRAINING	25 "
14.	PRACTICAL GYMNASTICS WITHOUT A TEACHER	25 "
15.	SPALDING'S LACROSSE RULES	10 "

Any of the above books mailed upon receipt of price.

Spalding's Complete Catalogue for 1888.

We have just issued our complete catalogue for 1888, containing nearly 500 separate illustrations of various articles used in every known sport, together with a carefully prepared price list and description of each article. We have endeavored to make the illustration and description so plain that customers from a distance can select an article quite as intelligently as if they had called at our Chicago or New York stores in person. In addition to its value as a catalogue, it contains a complete and valuable set of Sporting Rules, embracing Athletic Sports, Archery, Badminton, Bagatelle, Bicycling, Billiards, Pool, Boating, Boxing, Bowling, Caledonian Games, Club Swinging, Cricket, Croquet, Curling, Fly Casting, Foot Ball, Fencing, Gymnastics, Hand Ball, Lawn Tennis, Lacrosse, Polo, Quoits, Racquet, Running, Shooting, Skating, Walking, Wrestling Rules. This catalogue mailed to any address on receipt of 10 cents to cover postage.

These catalogues can be obtained of any of our Depots of Supplies, local agencies or direct from

SPALDING'S
Base Ball and Sporting Goods

FOR the convenience of patrons and for the purpose of bringing our complete line of Base Ball and Athletic Goods more prominently before Base Ball Players and Sportsmen generally, we have established the following Depots of Supplies in the leading cities throughout the United States, where will be found a complete line of Spalding's Base Ball Supplies, Lawn Tennis, Fishing Tackle, Bicycles, Foot Balls, Lacrosse, Cricket, Boxing Gloves, Indian Clubs, Fencing and all kinds of Gymnasium Goods and Apparatus, Worsted and Flannel Uniforms, Athletic Shoes and General Sporting Goods. These Depots are prepared to furnish our complete line of goods and specialties on equally as favorable terms as if ordered direct from our Chicago and New York houses. Orders for goods can be sent to

A. G. SPALDING & BROS.

108 Madison Street, - 241 Broadway

CHICAGO. NEW YORK.

Or any of the following **DEPOTS OF SUPPLIES**:

PADDOCK & VINE, 1 Green Street, Albany, N. Y.
SALEM G. LeVALLEY, 189 Main Street, Buffalo, N. Y.
J. R. HAWLEY, 164 Vine Street, Cincinnati, O.
VAN EPPS & CO., 259 Superior Street, Cleveland, O.
GEO. F. HIGGINS & CO., 354 16th Street, Denver, Col.
J. B. FIELD & CO., 77 Woodward Avenue, Detroit, Mich.
G. B. GROSVENOR, 744-752 Main Street, Dubuque, Ia.
V. KINDLER, 418 Genessee Avenue, East Saginaw, Mich.
A. J. ANDERSON, 2d and Houston Streets, Fort Worth, Texas
E. G. STUDLEY & CO., 4 Monroe Street, Grand Rapids, Mich.

E. E. MENGES & CO., 540 Delaware St., Kansas City, Mo.
J. W. RECCIUS & BRO., 304 Market Street, Louisville, Ky.
R. M. MANSFORD, 298 Main Street, Memphis, Tenn.
WEST BOOK & STATIONERY CO., 379 Broadway, Milwaukee, Wis.
F. A. LELAND, 426 Nicollet Avenue, Minneapolis, Minn.
F. F. HANSELL & BRO., 28 and 30 Camp St., New Orleans, La.
COLLINS GUN CO., 1312 Douglas Street, Omaha, Neb.
A. G. PRATT & CO., 79 5th Avenue, Pittsburgh, Pa.
WM. BECK & SON, 165-167 2d Street, Portland, Oregon.
RHODE ISLAND NEWS CO., 113 Westminster St., Providence, R.I.
SCRANTOM, WETMORE & CO., 10 State Street, Rochester, N. Y.
M. F. KENNEDY & BROS., 66 E. 3d Street, St. Paul, Minn.
E. C. MEACHAM ARMS CO., 515-517 Wash. Ave., St. Louis, Mo.
R. WOOD'S SONS, 72 and 74 S. Salina Street, Syracuse, N. Y.
M. A. TAPPAN, 819 Pennsylvania Avenue, Washington, D. C.
THE HINGSTON, SMITH ARMS CO., Winnipeg, Manitoba.
M. W. BULL, 445 Main Street, Springfield, Mass.
H. DREW & BRO., Jacksonville, Fla.
M. C. EBBECKE & CO., Allentown, Pa.

Spalding's Complete Catalogue of Base Ball and Athletic Goods, containing rules governing over 30 different sports, will be mailed upon application to any of the above, upon receipt of 10 cents to cover postage.

LOCAL AGENCIES.

In addition to our "Depots of Supplies," who do both a wholesale and retail business, we have established Local Agencies in the following cities, where ll line of our Base Ball and Athletic Goods will We hav rried, and where they are prepared to furnish o separate prices as charged at our Chicago and New ether with ores.

have
A. G. CASE, Aurora, Ill.
tom
C. E. DALTON, Bloomington, Ill.
y h
A. P. CUNNINGHAM, Champaign, Ill.
value
C. H. CARYL, Kalamazoo, Mich.
les,
SPENCER BROS. Marquette, Mich.
z,
FRANK PERCY, Oshkosh, Wis.
in
BUKER & SKINNER, Rockford, Ill.
m
BAKER & WATSON, Terre Haute, Ind.
n
McNIE & CO., Winona, Minn.
ilea
TUFTS-LYONS ARMS CO., Los Angeles, Cal.

"Spalding's Base Ball Guide" again greets the base ball public with the official records of America's national game. First issued in 1877, it has grown in popularity, has been enlarged and improved from year to year, and is now the recognized authority upon base ball matters. The statistics contained in the "Guide" can be relied upon, nearly all of them having been compiled from official records.

The "Guide" has attained such a size—180 pages—as to preclude the possibility of publishing in the same issue the League Constitution in full, and other interesting League matter. We are therefore compelled, in addition, to publish the "Official League Book," which contains only official League matter as furnished by Secretary Young, including the League Constitution in full.

Copies of the "Guide" or "League New York" be mailed to any address upon receipt of ten cents each. Trade orders supplied through the New Companies, or direct from the publishers.

CHICAGO. **A. G. SPALDING & BROS.** NEW YORK.

WASHINGTON, D. C., March 3, 1888.

By the authority vested in me, I do hereby certify that Messrs. A. G. Spalding & Bros., of Chicago and New York, have been granted the *exclusive* right to publish the Official League Book for 1888.

N. E. YOUNG,

Secretary National League of Professional Base Ball Clubs

AND

Official League Book for 1888.

A COMPLETE HAND BOOK OF THE NATIONAL GAME OF BASE BALL,

CONTAINING

STATISTICAL REVIEWS OF THE VARIOUS PROFESSIONAL ASSOCIATION CHAMPIONSHIP SEASONS, AS ALSO THE RECORDS AND AVERAGES OF THE INTER-COLLEGIATE ASSOCIATIONS, EAST AND WEST.

ADDED TO WHICH IS THE

COMPLETE OFFICIAL LEAGUE RECORD FOR 1887

TOGETHER WITH

THE NEW CODE OF PLAYING RULES, AS REVISED BY T born a wh COMMITTEE OF CONFERENCE. lished TTACHED TO WHICH IS AN OFFICIAL EXPLANATORY APPENDIX, GIVIN CORRECT INTERPRETATION OF THE NEW RULES, ALSO THE OFFICIAL RECORD OF ALL LEAGUE GAMES AND PLAYERS, AND THE OFFICIAL SCHEDULE OF LEAGUE GAMES FOR 1888; PITCHERS' RECORDS IN VICTORIES FOR 1887; RECORDS OF THE VETERAN BATSMEN OF THE LEAGUE FROM 1876 TO 1887.

PUBLISHED BY

A. G. SPALDING & BROS.

CHICAGO AND NEW YORK.

Entered according to Act of Congress, in the year 1888, by A. G. Spalding & Bros., in the

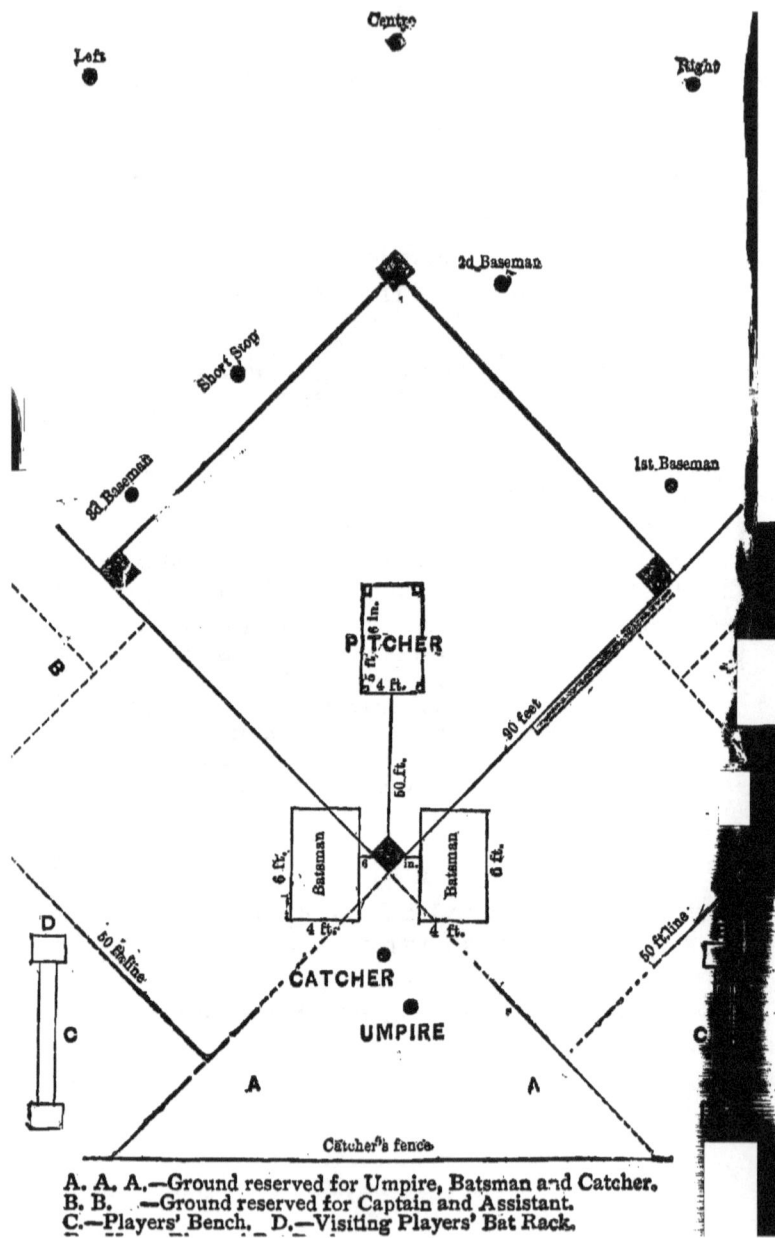

A. A. A.—Ground reserved for Umpire, Batsman and Catcher.
B. B.   —Ground reserved for Captain and Assistant.
C.—Players' Bench. D.—Visiting Players' Bat Rack.

ADRIAN C. ANSON.

Following a precedent established when the publication of SPALDING'S OFFICIAL BASE BALL GUIDE was first begun, we this year give that prominence to the champion batter of 1887, to which his superb work has entitled him. Capt. Adrian C. Anson, whom M. J. Kelly of the Boston Club characterizes as "the greatest base ball captain the country has produced," leads the batting list of 1887 with the remarkable percentage of .421. In this connection it is fair to remark that Maul, of the Philadelphia Club, has a percentage of .450. Maul, however, played in but sixteen games, while Anson played in 122 games. The fact that Maul did not play one-seventh as many games as Anson should not be ignored, and our readers will readily perceive why every consideration of justice demands that an average rating of a player should be made on a season's work, rather than on the record made during three weeks in a season.

Capt. Anson's face and figure are familiar to a large proportion of the quarter million of persons who will make a study as well as a reference book of the OFFICIAL GUIDE. For the benefit of the younger generation of base ball players and for the information of all admirers of the national game, it may be said in passing that the Captain who is known as "the old man," is not yet old in years while at heart he is "one of the boys." Blunt, frank, fearless, outspoken and sometimes very plainspoken is 'Cap.' Anson, but he is a man of convictions and he talks as he bats straight from the shoulder.

Base ball has developed some strong individual characters
is country, but it is doubtful whether any one player will ev
ave a deeper impress of personality on the sport than the powe
ul hitter, the clever disciplinarian, and the alert tacticion wh
oes into history as the champion batter of 1887. Subjoined
is record since 1876—the year the League was organized:

ear.	Position.	Averag
76	Fifth	3
77	Fourth	3
78	Fifth	3
79	First	4
80	Second	3
81	First	3
82	Second	3
83	Second	4
84	Fourth	3
85	Sixth	3
86	Second	3
87	First	4

The biographical record of Capt. Anson has been printed
equently in these pages, that it is only needful to say that he
native of Marshalltown, Iowa, and that he first played ball wi
e Forest City Club of Rockford, Ill., in 1871.

Equally deserving of mention in this chronicle, are the oth
reat hitters who have carried the leading distinction of first plac
he list of champion batsmen tabulated is as follows:

EAR.	NAME.	AVERAG
76	Ross Barnes	4
77	James White	3
78	A. Dalrymple	3
79	A. C. Anson	4
80	Geo. F. Gore	3
81	A. C. Anson	3
82	Dan Brouthers	3
83	Dan Brouthers	3
84	James O'Rourke	3
85	Roger Connor	3
86	M. J. Kelly	3
87	A. C. Anson	4

The foregoing figures tell their own story. There is a range
I points between the record made in 1884 and 1887. Althoug
e pitching has undergone a complete and radical evolution, tl
atting ability of the giant hitters seems to keep pace with the d
very It is certainly remarkable to contrast the average of Barn

INTRODUCTION.

It is now over a quarter of a century since the game of base ball became popularized as the game of games for American youth; and within that period it has so extended itself in its sphere of operations that it is now the permanently established national field game of America. Unlike many sports taken up by our people, which have ridden into general favor on the wave of a public furore, base ball has come to stay. Not even the great war of the rebellion could check its progress to any great extent; in fact, in one way—through the national army—it led to its being planted in a Southern clime, and now base ball can be said to "know no North, no South, no East, no West." It has even crossed the border into Canada, and in addition, like cricket, has found its way at times to foreign shores. Within the past fifteen years, too, the national game has burst its youthful bonds, and from the amateur period of its early growth it has entered upon the more advanced condition of its career under the professional system, which system has developed its innate attractions within a single decade to an extent it otherwise could not have reached in thrice the amount of time. In 1871 the first professional association was established, and now, in 1888, we find the professional fraternity, after their passage through the Red Sea of gambling abuses, so thoroughly controlled in the interests of honest play, by the existing professional organizations, that the evils which attach themselves to professionalism, in sports generally, no longer find space for existence within the arena of professional base ball playing. In fact, our national game now stands alone as a field sport in the one important fact that it is the only public sport in which professional exemplars take part which possesses the power to attract its thousands of spectators without the extrinsic aid of gambling. It is very questionable whether there is any public sport in the civilized portion of the world so eminently fitted for the people it was made for as the American national game of base ball. In every respect is it an outdoor sport admirably adapted for our mercurial population. It is full of excitement, is quickly played, and it not only requires vigor of constitution and a healthy physique, but manly courage, steady nerve, plenty of pluck, and considerable powers of judgment to excel in it.

What can present a more attractive picture to the lover of outdoor sports than the scene presented at a base ball match between two trained professional teams competing for championship honors, in which every point of play is so well looked after in the field, that it is only by some extra display of skill at the bat, or a lucky act of base-running at an opportune moment, that a single run is obtained in a full nine innings game? To watch the progress of a contest in which only one run is required to secure an important lead, and, while the game is in such a position, to see hit after hit made to the field, either in the form of high fly balls splendidly caught on the run by some active out-fielder, or a sharp ground hit beautifully picked up in the in-field, and swiftly and accurately thrown to the right baseman in time, is to see the perfection of base ball fielding, and that surpasses the fielding of every other known game of ball. Then there is the intense excitement incident to a contest in which one side is endeavoring to escape a "whitewash," while the other side as eagerly strives to retain their lead of a single run; and with the game in such position, a three base hit sends the runner to third base before a single hand is out, only to see the hit left unrewarded by the expected run, owing to the telling effect of the strategic pitching, and the splendid field support given it. Add to this the other excitement of a high hit over the out-fielder's head, made while two or three of the bases are occupied with the result of a tie score, or the securing of a lead at a critical point of the game, and a culmination of attractive features is reached, incidental to no other field game in vogue. If it is considered, too, that the pursuit of base ball is that of a healthy, recreative exercise, alike for the mind and body, suitable to all classes of our people, and to the adult as well as the mere boy, there can be no longer room for surprise that such a game should reach the unprecedented popularity that the American game of base ball has attained.

THE PROFESSIONAL SEASON OF 1887.

The professional season of 1887 stands forth as "the best on record," in regard to the vast number of people who patronized the championship contests from April to October of that year. Unfortunately we have no official statistics at command, from which to ascertain the exact number of spectators gathered at the ball contests of the professional clubs in 1887; but judging from the attendance at the principal matches played by the League and American Association clubs during their respective championship seasons, the crowds can be easily reckoned by the hundred thousands. Besides the immense aggregate of people who patronized the professional clubs, the great holiday gatherings also beat all previous records known in the history of the game, there never having been so many people at a ball match in either New York or Brooklyn, since the national game was established, as there were on Decoration Day, 1887, when over thirty thousand people entered the Polo grounds to see the championship matches between the Chicago and New York club teams, and over twenty thousand the matches at Washington Park the same day between the St. Louis champions and the Brooklyn club team, both of the local teams being handsomely defeated by the visiting club teams.

In regard to the championship campaigns of the two leading professional organizations it may be said that while that of the National League proved to be unusually interesting, that of the American Association was one sided almost from the start. But two of the prominent professional associations of the season of 1887, went through the campaign without a club break in their club ranks, and these were the National League and the American Association, the Inter-national League failing to go through the season as creditably as it did in 1886, while the New England League failed to go through with the programme laid down for it in the spring, as did the Southern League and the Eastern League, the latter making a very bad break. The trouble was largely due to the lack of judgment shown by the minor Association clubs in the laying out of paying circuits for one thing, and secondly from their engaging to pay higher salaries to their team players than their capital and their facilities for obtaining remunerative returns warranted. With all these drawbacks, however, the professional season, as a whole, was a financial success, especially in the case of the best managed club teams.

The record of the professional season of 1887 may be summed up in brief as follows:

Leagues.	Winning Club.	Games Played.	Began the Season.	Ended the Season.
National League...............	Detroit............	492	8 Clubs	8 Clubs
American Association.........	St. Louis.........	536	8 "	8 "
Northwestern League..........	Oshkosh...........	481	8 "	8 "
International League..........	Toron o..	474	8 "	7 "
Western League	Topeka............	374	8 "	6 "
New England League..........	Lowell............	351	8 "	5 "
Southern League...............	New Orleans....	273	6 "	4 "
Eastern League................	Waterbury.......	167	6 "	2 "
California League.............	Pioneer..........	......	3 "	3 "

THE LEAGUE SEASON OF 1887.

Beyond question the National League season of 1887 was the most successful one known in the eleven years' history of the organization. Not only were the financial returns in the aggregate the largest ever received, but the pennant race was the most closely contested of any since the League was established. The only drawback to the season's success may be said to be the bad field management which marked the running of the majority of the teams of the league. The campaign opened very promisingly for a material change of issues from the hitherto rather one sided result which had characterized the pennant races of 1885 and 1886, inasmuch as the changes which had taken place in the make up of the Chicago team for 1887 had greatly lessened that club's chances for continued success in the championship arena, while the added strength to the Boston Club's team had made that team quite a favorite in the then coming race. Then, too, there was the Detroit Club, with its strong team, as a very promising candidate for championship honors, while Philadelphia stood ready to improve their pennant race record under the auspices of the most experienced manager in the league. New York had its usual Spring anticipations in regard to its league club, but it was on the principle of "hoping for the best while prepared for the worst." The new element of the campaign was the newly entered candidates for league honors from Pittsburg and Indianapolis, which two clubs replaced the St. Louis and Kansas City clubs. Nothing was expected from either club likely to disturb the prominent teams in the race; but as it turned out they both proved to be important factors in the calculations of the campaign, for though these clubs with the reconstructed Washington team, were the three tail enders in the race, they materially aided in making the pennant contest interesting, Pittsburg proving to be a thorn in the path of Chicago, while Washington materially interfered with the success of New York, and Indianapolis with that of Boston. Almost from the beginning of last year's race there were really but four competitors in the contest, the other four being little else than make weights. At the outset Detroit, Philadelphia, and Boston, started the race with a good burst of speed, New York also being among the leaders, while Chicago and Pittsburg comparatively were outsiders. By the middle of the season, however, Chicago had rallied in fine style, but Philadelphia had lost valuable ground. Before two-thirds of the season had ended the places for the four leaders had been picked out, and they were accepted; and neither Boston nor Pittsburg were included—the tail-enders had been Washington and Indianapolis from the start—Detroit, Chicago, Philadelphia, and New York being the "big four" of the pennant race of 1887.

THE CHAMPIONSHIP CAMPAIGN.

Not since the League season of 1883 has there been as close and exciting a race for the League championship pennant as during the past season of 1887. The circumstances attendant upon the entries for the race were of such an exceptional character as to impart a new interest to the contest; inasmuch as there were not only two new candidates for championship honors in the League field in 1887, but the partial breaking up of the old regular team of the Chicago club, and the transfer of one of the leading players of that team to the Boston club, led to new calculations in regard to the probable issue of the campaign, and to such an extent as to greatly increase the public interest in the pennant race of the season. The new competitors for League honors were the Pittsburg and Indianapolis clubs, these taking the place of the retiring St. Louis and Kansas City clubs. The advent of the Pittsburg club in the League was regarded as a decided gain to the ranks of the Senior professional organization; and the Pittsburg people were sanguine of seeing their pet club take a leading position in the pennant race, as that club in the American race of the previous season had come in a close second to the famous St. Louis team, the world's champions of 1886. In regard to the Indianapolis club no such expectations were looked forward to with any hope of realization; though with the strong players they had in their team a good position in the race was anticipated by their friends; but the wretched management the club team was subjected to in the earlier part of the season proved to be too heavy a handicap for them in the race, and despite a good rally under better leadership in the closing months of the campaign, they finally had to submit to the occupancy of the tail end position in the race.

THE CHAMPIONSHIP CAMPAIGN RECORD.

The campaign of 1887 opened on April 28, the New York and Philadelphia clubs leading off in the East, and the Detroit and Indianapolis clubs in the West, rain preventing the appointed games at Washington and Pittsburg, where the Boston and Chicago clubs were to have played on that date. By the middle of May, Detroit had obtained a leading position in the race, with Boston a good second, Philadelphia third and New York fourth, Pittsburg standing fifth, while Chicago—hitherto prominently in the van each season at the very outset—had to be contented with sixth position, Washington and Indianapolis bringing up the rear. The end of the May campaign saw but little change in the relative positions of the contesting teams, except that New York had pushed ahead of Philadelphia, and Chicago led Pittsburg, Detroit still being in the van, and Boston a good second. In June Chicago began their uphill fight for a leading position, their plucky work in this respect proving to be the feature of the campaign; and by the middle of June they had not only passed Pittsburg, but had left Philadelphia in the rear, and from this time out they occupied one of the four leading positions in the race. The end of June saw the Detroits still in the van, with the Bostons a good second, New York third and Chicago a close fourth—Philadelphia, Pittsburg, Washington and Indianapolis following in the order named. Up to the close of the first week in July, Detroit had not only taken the lead in the race from the outset, but Boston had occupied second place and New York third, with but a trifling change in their relative positions each month; but now Boston and New York both began to drop back, while Chicago kept forcing its way up close to Detroit, the record of July 5 seeing Chicago in third place ahead of New York, while the record of July 11 saw the Bostons retire from second place in the race and the Chicago team take up the position, Philadelphia still remaining fifth, with Pittsburg, Washington and Indianapolis in the rear. The end of July saw Chicago a close second to Detroit, with Bostons third. Washington marked this month by getting ahead of Pittsburg, the latter team on July 30, occupying seventh position in the race. The relative position of the contestants in the race was not changed until the last week in August, by which time the Chicago team were tie with Detroit on record of victories. Philadelphia began to pull up in this month, and by the 20th had passed Boston, and was closing up with New York, the Boston team equaling New York's record by the 27th. By the second week in September, Philadelphia drove New York out of third position, and began to give Chicago a close race for second place, the champions falling off in their play considerably the latter part of this month.

By the middle of September Detroit had virtually secured first place in the race, so much so, indeed, that all the interest now centered in the contest for second place which Chicago, Philadelphia and New York were striving to reach. Before the month ended, however, New York apparently retired from the fight for second place, and only hoped to retain third position. But October's games saw Philadelphia jump into second place, leaving Chicago in third position, and New York had to be content with fourth place and Boston with fifth, the ending of the campaign being a sad disappointment to the Bostons, who after all the large outlay incurred for star players, found their team in no higher position at the end of the season of 1887, than that the team of 1886 had occupied, though their record of victories was greater by 61 to 56, and their defeats fewer by 60 to 61; Pittsburg had improved upon St. Louis by 55 victories to 43, and Indianapolis upon Kansas City by 37 victories to 30. But the greatest jump was that of Washington from 28 victories in 1886 to 46 in 1887. New York fell back from their 1886 record by 68 victories this year against 75 in 1886, while Philadelphia improved from 71 in 1886 to 75 in 1887. Both Chicago and Detroit, however, failed to equal their 1886 record, Detroit falling off 8 games and Chicago 11.

THE LESSONS OF THE LEAGUE CAMPAIGN.

Three results of the championship campaign of the League for 1887, call for special comment, and these are, first the notable success of the Detroit team in winning the pennant; secondly, the remarkable success achieved by the Chicago team under the peculiar circumstances of their entering the lists as they did; and thirdly, the noteworthy failure of the Boston club after entering upon the campaign as they did with the advantages they had purchased at such a large financial outlay. To these may be added the steady progress toward the goal of the championship made by the admirably managed Philadelphia team, which last season reached a point nearer the capture of the pennant than the club ever before attained. The success of the Detroits, introducing, as it does, a new possessor of championship honors, may justly be regarded as an advantage to the general interests of the National League. It is not desirable that one club should season after season carry off the honors, as the old Boston team did in the early period of the professional championship contests. Nor has it been advantageous that Chicago has been able to monopolize the lead as it has done within the past decade. Up to 1887 but three clubs out of the eight which have each year entered for the League pennant have been able to win the championship, and these three were Chicago,

Boston and Providence, the two first named monopolizing the lead. This necessarily has lessened the interest taken in the annual competition, besides which it has materially interfered with the financial success of the majority of the contesting teams. Now that the Chicago Club has been forced to occupy a secondary position, and a club new to championship honors has taken its place, the other unsuccessful teams will begin to entertain hopes of "getting in at the death" in future pennant races, and thereby a new interest will be imparted to future championship campaigns.

The surprisingly good work accomplished by the "weakened Chicago team"—as it was called—in this year's campaign, is a result which calls for the most earnest consideration of the question of insisting upon strict temperance in the ranks for the National League season of 1888. The evil of drunkenness among the professional teams is one which has grown upon the fraternity until it has become too costly an abuse to be longer tolerated. Drunken professionals should be driven from service just as the crooks of a dozen years ago were, never to be allowed to return. Drunken players are not only a costly drawback to success individually, but they permeate the whole baseball fraternity with a demoralizing influence. The fact is, professional baseball playing has arrived at that point of excellence, and reached so advanced a position in regard to its financial possibilities, that it will no longer pay, in any solitary respect, to allow players of drinking habits in first-class teams. The demands of the game, as it is now played, are such as to require a player to have all his wits about him to play ball up to the standard it has now reached. He needs the steadiest of nerves, the clearest eyesight, the most unclouded judgment, and the healthiest physique to play the game as it is required to be done by the exacting public patrons of the present day. Another thing, the capitalists who have ventured thousands of dollars in baseball stock companies, can no longer allow their money to be risked in teams which are weakened by the presence of men of drinking habits. Mr. Spalding's plucky and most successful experiment has conclusively shown that a baseball team run on temperance principles can successfully compete with teams stronger in other respects, but which are weakened by the toleration of drinking habits in their ranks. Here is a lesson taught by the campaign of 1887 which points a moral, if it does not adorn a tale.

The third lesson of the campaign is that taught by the Boston Club's experience, and that is that one "star" does not make a team; nor can the pennant be won by any costly outlay in securing the services of this, that or the other "greatest player in the country." It is well managed and harmonious teams, not picked nines led by special stars, which win in the long run. Now and then—as there are exceptions in all cases—a picked nine will attain a certain degree of success. But for steady struggles for permanent success in the professional championship arena, team work of the very best, and admirably managed teams will alone achieve steady victory. The old Boston teams under Harry Wright, and the Chicago teams under Anson are a standing proof of this fact. Let the National League magnates ponder these truths earnestly before they meet in convention next December.

THE SEASON'S RECORD FOR 1887.

The following table presents a very complete statistical table of the work done by the eight Leagues in the championship campaign of 1887. It presents the figures of every important feature of the championship series of games from April to October, inclusive.

	Detroit.	Philadelphia.	Chicago.	New York.	Boston.	Pittsburg.	Washington.	Indianapolis.	Totals.
Victories........................	79	75	71	68	61	55	46	37	492
Defeats...........................	45	48	50	55	60	69	76	89	492
Games Played..................	124	123	121	123	121	124	122	126	....
Per Cent. of Victories.........	.637	.610	.587	.553	.504	.444	.377	.294	...
Drawn Games..................	2	5	4	6	3	1	4	1	26
Series Won......................	6	4	6	4	3	2	0	1	26
Series Lost......................	1	2	1	3	3	4	6	6	26
Series Tied......................	0	1	0	0	1	1	1	0	4
Victories at Home.............	44	38	44	36	39	31	26	24	282
Victories Abroad...............	35	37	27	32	22	24	20	13	210
Defeats at Home...............	17	23	18	26	22	33	32	39	210
Defeats Abroad.................	28	25	32	29	38	36	44	50	282
"Chicago" Victories............	3	7	4	5	4	4	3	4	34
"Chicago" Defeats..............	2	2	2	5	5	6	6	6	34
Victories in Ten Innings Games.	1	3	0	2	3	2	4	3	18
In Eleven Innings Games..	1	0	0	0	0	1	1	0	3
In Twelve " " ..	0	0	1	0	0	0	0	1	2
In Thirteen " " ..	1	0	0	0	0	1	0	0	2
In Fourteen " " ..	0	1	0	0	0	0	0	0	1
Double Figure Victories.......	38	28	24	21	23	8	10	14	166
Single Figure Victories........	41	47	47	47	38	47	36	23	326
Double Figure Defeats.........	17	18	16	19	20	20	25	31	166
Single Figure Defeats..........	28	30	34	36	30	39	51	58	326
Games Won by One Run......	8	14	13	19	9	17	13	13	104
Games Lost by One Run......	11	11	11	13	15	13	14	10	104
Highest Score in a Game.....	21	24	19	29	28	23	23	18	....
Batting Average.................	.350	.321	.321	.330	.323	.280	.285	.293	....
Fielding Average................	.926	.919	.910	.918	.897	.917	.912	.913	....

LEAGUE CHAMPIONSHIP STATISTICS FOR 1887.

The statistics of the League championship campaign for 1887 present a series of very interesting figures, prominent among which are the records of the double figure and single figure victories and defeats scored by each of the eight League clubs from April 28 to October 8, inclusive. The record of single figure victories shows not only good fielding but effective battery work, while the double figure victories indicate less effective pitching and fielding and freer batting. Only 166 games of the League championship series were marked by single figure victories, and, singularly enough, Detroit excelled in this respect, while in double figure victories—of which there were no less than 326 in the series—Detroit stood fifth on the list, whereas it was expected that in this kind of game they would take a decided lead. Pittsburg was the last on the list in scoring single figure victories, both Indianapolis and Washington leading the former club in this respect; but in double victories Pittsburg led the Detroit "sluggers," this title being apparently a misnomer for the Detroits, so far as it indicates heavy batting. In the "slugging" business—as shown by the home run record—Chicago took a decided lead, while Detroit stood a bad second and Boston a good third, and yet Detroit won the pennant, Chicago was third in the race and Boston fifth. This would show pretty plainly that "slugging" in batting, as opposed to scientific batting, is not an element of success in pennant winning. In double figure defeats Detroit had the fewest, thereby showing effective work in the box, Philadelphia being second and Chicago third. In single figure defeats, too, Detroit, Philadelphia and Chicago had the fewest. The records given below include the "Chicago" games, of which there were four with double figure scores on one side and twenty-nine with single figures.

The table showing the double and single figure victories and defeats scored by the eight League clubs in the championship series of games of 1887, is as follows: The letter D is for the double figure games, and the letter S for the single figure.

	Detroit.		Philadelphia.		Chicago.		New York.		Boston.		Pittsburg.		Washington.		Indianapolis.		Total Victories.		T'l Victories.
	D	S	D	S	D	S	D	S	D	S	D	S	D	S	D	S	Double.	Single.	
Detroit......			6	4	4	4	3	7	4	7	7	6	9	4	5	9	38	41	79
Philadelphia	4	4			3	3	4	6	3	6	1	11	4	9	9	8	28	47	75
Chicago.....	3	7	4	8			4	7	4	5	1	4	5	6	3	10	24	47	71
New York...	4	4	2	5	1	5			1	9	3	9	2	8	8	7	21	47	68
Boston.	3	4	4	5	1	5	4	3			4	7	2	8	5	6	23	38	61
Pittsburg....	1	3	1	5	3	9	1	5	2	5			0	9	0	11	8	47	54
Washington	0	4	1	2	3	4	1	7	3	4	1	8			1	7	10	36	46
Indianapolis	2	2	0	1	1	4	2	1	3	4	3	4	3	7			14	23	37
Games Lost.	17	28	18	30	16	34	19	36	20	40	20	39	25	51	31	58	166	326	492

THE FIELDING OF 1887.

Of the four distinct features of the national game of base ball viz: *pitching*, *batting*, *fielding* and *base running*, skilful play in handling the ball in the field is beyond question the most attractive. It is something all can appreciate and understand. While scientific batting is only appreciable by those who fully understand the difficulties attendant upon it, fine play in the field can be enjoyed by every spectator, its beauties being as plainly apparent as is the characteristic blundering in the field of a mere novice in the art. In batting, however, while the great majority fully enjoy the dashing, splurgy, long-hit ball which yields a home run, it is only the minority who have sufficient knowledge of the "points" in the game to appreciate the scientific work of "facing for position," "timing the swing of the bat," "observing good form," and other like points in team-work at the bat. But in fielding, every one in general crowd of spectators knows when a fine "pick-up" of a hot grounder is made; or when a hot "liner" is handsomely caught on the fly; or a short high ball is held after a long run in for it from the outer field; or when an apparently safe hit to right field is changed into an out at first base by the active fielding and quick accurate throwing in of the ball to the first baseman by the right-fielder. Then, too, the brilliant catching of the swift curved line balls from the pitcher by the catcher, and the splendid throwing of the latter to the bases; all these features of sharp and skilful fielding are evidences of good work which the veriest novice in the crowd can understand and appreciate. Hence it is that fielding is at once the most brilliant and attractive feature of base-ball. Fielding has made rapid strides toward perfection within the past decade, and especially within the past three years. There is more system about it than there used to be. Last year, for instance, saw more of that special element of success in fielding—good "backing-up"—exhibited, than ever before. There was more "playing for the side," too, in the fielding of 1887 than in any previous season's work; and this important matter of playing for the side, is far more frequently seen in fielding than in batting. In batting, the rule is to play for one's individual record, because playing for the side is more self-sacrificing in batting than in fielding. In fielding, you really help your record more by playing for the side than for a special record; hence, "playing for the side" is necessarily more practiced in handling the ball than in wielding the bat.

THE BATTING OF 1887.

Though the batting done in 1887 was to a certain extent an improvement over that of the year before, still the fact remains that in batting the players of the present have more to learn than in any other department of the game. Scientific batting—which is neither more nor less than doing team work at the bat such as in "placing the ball," making "sacrifice hits," studying the philosophy of handling the bat in proper form against strategic pitching—is as yet known only to a minority of batsmen. In regard to the features of scientific batting it may be said that the highest degree of skill in handling the bat is reached when the batsman can "place a ball"—sent in by swift curved-line pitching in any part of the field he chooses. It is, however, the most difficult of all batting feats which a batsman can attempt. There are so many points to be learned so as to become thoroughly familiar with them, before this placing of a ball can be accomplished, that it is rarely that one sees this finishing touch in the art of batting exhibited. But when it is at command, what an immense advantage it gives the batsman in outwitting his fielding opponents, and what an aid it is in sending runners round from first base to home base. Then it is that the necessity for making the placing of a ball a feature of a batsman's works becomes plainly apparent. When the professional fraternity have gone through the "slugging" era, and the ambition to excel in the home-run style of batting has been superseded by more scientific work in handling the ash, the coming batsmen of the future will look back with surprise to think that they should, for so many years have attended only to the weakest method of batting.

All batsmen who go in for a record strive their utmost to make home runs. They are well aware of the fact that the majority of spectators at a match—especially in country towns—know little or nothing of what constitutes real skill in batting; the prevailing idea with the crowd being, that the best batsman is the "slugger" who manages to scratch a home run once out of every nine times at the bat. Hence the eclat attendant upon a dashing hit of the kind is too tempting to resist, and hence they throw team work in batting to the dogs, and go in for a style of batting which pleases the crowd, though it proves costly in the long run to the success of a team in taking the lead in a championship race. A glance at the cost of a home run in wear and tear of a batsman's physical strength, will show what a drawback the slugging style of batting is in progress toward scientific hitting and thorough team work at the bat.

THE "CHICAGO" GAMES OF 1887.

The record of the "Chicago" games—or games in which the defeated team did not score a single run—in the League championship series of 1887 is appended:

	Philadelphia	Chicago	Detroit	New York	Boston	Pittsburg	Indianapolis	Washington	Won
Philadelphia		0	0	1	2	1	3	0	7
New York	1	0	0		1	1	2	0	5
Chicago	0		0	0	0	1	0	3	4
Boston	1	1	1	1		0	0	0	4
Pittsburg	0	0	0	1	0		1	2	4
Indianapolis	0	0	0	0	1	2		1	4
Detroit	0	0		1	1	1	0	0	3
Washington	0	1	1	1	0	0	0		3
Lost	2	2	2	4	5	6	6	6	34

In 1886 there were 41 "Chicago" games played, Philadelphia leading with ten such victories; Chicago being second with eight, and Detroit third with six, St. Louis and Washington scoring four each, and Boston, New York and Kansas City three each.

THE SERIES RECORD OF 1887.

The following table presents the figures of the *series* of games won and lost in the League championship arena in 1887. The letters "W" and "L" mean won and lost.

	Detroit	Philadelphia	Chicago	New York	Boston	Pittsburg	Washington	Indianapolis	Series Won	Series Lost	Series Tied
	W. L.	W. L.	W. L.	W. L.	W. L.	W. L.	W. L.	W. L.			
Detroit	....	10.. 8	8..10	10.. 8	11.. 7	13 4	13.. 4	14.. 4	6	1	0
Philadelphia	8..10	......	6..12	10.. 7	9.. 9	12.. 6	13 .. 3	17.. 1	4	2	1
Chicago	10.. 8	12.. 6	......	11.. 6	9.. 6	5..12	11.. 7	13.. 5	6	1	0
New York	8..10	7..10	6..1	......	10.. 7	12.. 6	10.. 8	15.. 3	4	3	0
Boston	7..11	9.. 9	6.. 9	7..10	......	11.. 7	10.. 7	11.. 7	3	3	1
Pittsburg	4 13	6..12	12.. 5	6..12	7..11	......	9.. 9	11.. 7	2	4	1
Washington	4..13	3..13	7..11	8 10	7..10	9.. 9	......	8..10	0	6	1
Indianapolis	4..14	1 17	5..13	3..15	7..11	7..11	10.. 8	......	1	6	0

THE MONTHLY RECORDS.

One of the most interesting of the annual records of the championship campaign each year, is that showing the progress made by each of the eight clubs during each month of the championship season. These monthly records have been features of the *League Guide* some years now, and they are read with interest by all, for they tell a very instructive story of the changes experienced each week of the pennant race, from May until October. The eight League contestants in 1887 started out in the pennant race of '87 during the last three days of April, and the Detroits closed that month in the lead and without the loss of a game, as did Boston, New York closing third; and the end of May saw these three clubs occupying the same leading positions, the Detroit team ending the third week in May with the record of nineteen victories out of twenty-one games played, a record which gave them the prestige of victory at the very outset. Boston, too, opened the May campaign very promisingly, that team closing the month with a record of nineteen victories out of twenty-seven games. New York ended third with sixteen victories out of twenty-eight games; Philadelphia being a close fourth, while the champion Chicago team had to remain content with fifth place, and Pittsburg with sixth, the friends of the latter club expecting a far better showing on the part of that team. Of course, Washington and Indianapolis brought up the rear, the latter team's record being very poor, as they only won six games out of twenty-eight games played. Here is the joint record for April's three days and the month's figures for May.

APRIL AND MAY.

APRIL AND MAY.	April		1st wk		2d wk		3d wk		4th wk		5th wk		Totals		
	W.	L.	W.	L.	W.	L.	W.	L.	W.	L.	W.	L.	W.	L.	P.
Detroit.........	3	0	5	1	5	1	6	0	1	3	1	2	21	7	28
Boston.........	2	0	3	2	4	2	5	1	3	2	2	1	19	8	27
New York......	2	1	3	3	2	4	5	1	3	2	1	2	16	12	28
Philadelphia...	1	2	3	2	4	2	1	5	4	1	2	1	15	13	28
Chicago........	0	1	1	4	4	2	2	4	2	3	2	1	11	15	26
Pittsburg.......	1	0	3	2	2	4	1	5	2	1	1	2	10	14	24
Washington....	0	2	1	4	2	4	3	3	1	1	1	1	8	15	23
Indianapolis...	0	3	2	4	1	5	1	5	1	4	1	1	6	22	28
Totals.........	9	9	21	21	24	24	24	24	17	17	11	11	106	106	

JUNE.

The month's play in June saw the champions from Chicago begin their noted up-hill fight for first place; which proved to be one of the peculiar features of the League campaign of 1887, Detroit and Boston falling off after their opening spurt in May, while Philadelphia met with disastrous ill-luck in having players disabled. On the other hand, New York made a spurt in the running, and the result was that the latter team at the end of June stood next to Chicago in the month's record, while Philadelphia ran down to seventh. Only four of the eight clubs won more games than they lost this month, and they were Chicago, New York, Detroit and Boston, the Indianapolis team doing even worse than in May, as they only won seven games out of the twenty-one they played during June. Here is the record for June:

JUNE.	1st wk		2d wk		3d wk		4th wk		5th wk		Totals.		
	W.	L.	W.	L.	W.	L.	W.	L.	W.	L.	W.	L.	P.
Chicago	2	0	3	3	5	1	4	0	1	2	15	5	20
New York	2	2	3	2	4	3	3	1	2	1	14	9	23
Detroit	0	2	4	0	3	3	3	1	2	2	12	8	20
Boston	2	2	3	1	4	3	1	4	1	2	11	12	23
Pittsburg	2	1	2	3	2	4	1	3	3	1	9	12	21
Washington	2	1	2	2	2	4	1	3	2	2	9	12	21
Ph'ladelphia	1	3	1	4	3	3	1	3	3	1	9	14	23
Indianapolis	1	1	1	4	2	4	3	2	0	3	7	14	21
Totals	12	12	19	19	25	25	17	17	14	14	86	86	

JULY.

The feature of the July record was the continued success of the Chicago team, in keeping up their rally for the lead, and the good pull-up made by Philadelphia. Detroit just held their own, while New York lost as many games as they won, as did Boston, Washington showing up quite strong in July; while Pittsburgh only won nine out of twenty-five games, even Indianapolis doing better than the former. Chicago led with sixteen victories out of their twenty-four games in July, the fight for the pennant now being regarded as a battle between Detroit and Chicago, with New York a close competitor. Here is the July record:

JULY.	1st wk		2d wk		3d wk		4th wk		5th wk		Totals.		
	W.	L.	W.	L.	W.	L.	W.	L.	W.	L.	W.	L.	P.
Chicago	2	0	6	0	3	2	2	3	3	3	16	8	24
Philadelphia	0	2	2	4	5	0	3	2	3	2	13	10	23
Detroit	2	0	4	1	1	4	1	4	4	2	12	11	23
New York	2	0	1	5	1	4	4	0	3	2	11	11	22
Washington	0	2	1	4	5	1	3	2	2	3	11	12	23
Boston	2	0	2	3	3	2	2	1	1	4	10	10	20
Indianapolis	0	2	4	1	1	4	1	3	3	3	9	13	22
Pittsburg	0	2	2	4	2	4	2	3	3	3	9	16	25
Totals	8	8	22	22	21	21	18	18	22	22	91	91	

AUGUST.

By August the Philadelphias had rallied so as to have secured a position among the leaders again, and this month that team won seventeen games out of the twenty-one, thereby making the best record of the month. Detroit, too, had begun to make its club's position sure, while New York was talking about their club being a good candidate for second place at least. Pittsburg, too, in August, improved its position, that club's team for the first time winning more games than they lost, while Chicago did not do as well, and Boston lost more games than they won. Of course the Washington and Indianapolis teams brought up the rear, the latter's bad management during the first three months, culminating in August. Here is the record for that month:

AUGUST.	1st wk		2d wk		3d wk		4th wk		5th wk		Total.		
	W.	L.	W.	L.	W.	L.	W.	L.	W.	L.	W.	L.	P.
Philadelphia	3	2	4	1	4	1	4	1	2	3	17	8	25
Detroit	4	2	2	3	2	3	4	1	5	1	17	10	27
New York	3	2	2	3	3	2	3	2	3	2	14	11	25
Pittsburg	1	4	4	2	3	1	1	3	4	2	13	12	15
Chicago	4	2	3	2	2	3	1	2	2	2	12	11	23
Boston	3	3	2	2	2	4	2	0	3	3	12	13	25
Washington	2	3	2	3	2	4	2	5	2	3	10	18	28
Indianapolis	1	3	2	4	2	2	2	5	0	5	7	19	26
Totals	21	21	21	21	20	20	19	19	21	21	102	102	

SEPTEMBER.

The deciding month of the season proved to be September, and in this month the Detroit team virtually settled the championship question, and Philadelphia's brilliant rally for second position was the exciting feature of the month's play, that team winning sixteen games out of the twenty-one won and lost. Chicago fell off in their play owing to Pfeffer's failure to do good work, and New York lost valuable ground this month, that team winning but one more game than they lost in September. Boston, too, fell back in the race, showing none of the old rallying power previously so characteristic of that team's work, while Pittsburg lost no less than fifteen games out of the twenty-four played. Here is the month's record:

SEPTEMBER.	1st wk		2d wk		3d wk		4th wk		5th wk		Totals.		
	W.	L.	W.	L.	W.	L.	W.	L.	W.	L.	W.	L.	P.
Detroit	2	1	5	1	5	1	2	3	4	0	18	6	24
Philadelphia	1	1	5	1	3	3	5	0	2	0	16	5	21
Chicago	1	1	3	3	4	1	5	0	2	2	15	7	22
New York	1	2	2	3	3	2	4	2	2	2	12	11	23
Boston	3	0	3	2	3	3	1	4	1	2	11	11	22
Pittsburg	1	1	2	3	4	2	0	6	2	3	9	15	24
Washington	1	1	1	5	0	6	3	4	1	2	6	18	24
Indianapolis	0	3	1	4	1	5	5	4	0	3	5	19	24
Totals	10	10	22	22	23	23	23	23	14	14	92	92	

OCTOBER.

October saw the Detroit club virtually the victors in the championship race, and in that month they made no effort to improve their record, they leaving the week's play in October to settle the contest for second and third place. Philadelphia made a spurt at the finish and came in a good second, while Chicago managed to secure third place. New York obtained fourth, and Boston had to remain content with fifth position. In the week's play in October Pittsburg made a fine rally to recover their lost ground, but it was too late to be of service. The figures below tell the story of the work done in October, the contrast between the play of Philadelphia and Boston in October being especially noteworthy:

OCTOBER.	W.	L.	W.	L.	P.
Philadelphia	6	0	6	0	6
Pittsburg	6	1	6	1	7
Washington	3	3	3	3	6
Indianapolis	3	4	3	4	7
Chicago	3	5	3	5	8
New York	2	3	2	3	5
Detroit	2	4	2	4	6
Boston	1	6	1	6	7
Totals	26	26	26	26	

The following is the complete summary of each month's victories and defeats by months:

	April.		May.		June.		July.		Aug.		Sept.		Oct.		Totals.		
	W.	L.	W.	L.	W.	L.	W.	L.	W.	L.	W.	L.	W.	L.	W.	L.	P.
Detroit	3	0	18	7	12	8	11	11	15	9	18	6	2	4	79	45	124
Philadelphia	1	2	14	11	9	13	13	10	16	7	16	5	6	0	75	48	123
Chicago	0	1	11	14	15	5	16	8	11	10	15	7	3	5	71	50	121
New York	2	1	14	11	14	9	11	11	13	9	12	11	2	3	68	55	123
Boston	2	0	17	8	11	12	10	10	9	13	11	11	1	6	61	60	121
Pittsburg	1	0	9	14	9	12	9	16	11	11	10	15	6	1	55	69	124
Washington	0	2	8	13	9	12	11	11	9	16	6	19	3	3	46	76	122
Indianapolis	0	3	6	19	7	15	9	13	7	16	5	19	3	4	37	89	126
Totals	9	9	97	97	86	86	90	90	91	91	93	93	26	26	492	492	

EXTRA INNINGS GAMES.

The record of the victories and defeats scored by the eight League Clubs in extra innings games in the championship series of 1887, was as follows:

VICTORIES.

Date.	Contesting Clubs.	Cities.	Pitch'rs	Innings	Score.
June 25	Washington v. Pittsb'g	Pittsburg ..	Whitney......Galvin	11	5- 4
June 30	" v. Chicago	Chicago....	O'Day......Baldwin	10	4- 3
May 23	" v. Detroit	Washingt'n	Whitney.....Getzein	10	7- 6
June 29	" v. Pittsb'g	Pittsbugh...	Whitney..... Morris	10	7- 6
July 20	" v. Detroit	Washingt'n	Whitney...... Burke	10	9- 6
July 29	Philadelphia v. Pittsb'g	Pittsburg...	Buffinton McCormick	14	3- 2
July 26	" v. Wash'n	Washingt'n	Buffinton....Gilmore	10	6- 5
Aug. 16	" v. "	Philadelp'a	Ferguson.....O'Day	10	7- 6
Aug. 4	" v. Chicago	Chicago....	Casey......Baldwin	10	13- 9
Aug. 19	Pittsburg v. Chicago...	Pittsburg...	Galvin......Clarkson	13	6- 5
Aug. 9	" v. Boston....	Pittsburg...	Galvin....Radbourne	11	6- 5
Sept. 25	" v. Chicago...	Chicago....	Galvin......Clarkson	10	6- 5
July 25	" v. Indianap's	Pittsburg...	McCormick....Boyle	10	7- 6
June 16	Iudianapolis v. Pittsb'g	Indiana'olis	Kirby....McCormick	12	4- 2
Aug. 19	" v. Detroit.	Indiana'olis	Shreve......Conway	10	4- 1
May 23	" v. Boston..	Boston.....	Healy.....Radbourne	10	9- 8
June 23	" v. "	Indiana'olis	Morrison... Madden	10	10- 9
May 10	Detroit v. Pittsburg....	Pittsburg...	Weidman.....Galvin	13	6- 5
May 4	" v. "	Pittsburg...	Weidman.....Galvin	11	9- 8
May 30	" v. Boston........	Boston.....	Weidman Radbourne	10	2- 1
May 24	Boston v. Indianapolis.	Boston.....	Conway......Boyle	10	8- 7
Aug. 6	" v. Detroit.....	Detroit.....	Radbourne...Getzein	10	11-10
June 17	" v. New York..	Boston.....	Conway...Matthews	10	19- 9
July 22	N. Y. v. Indianapolis..	New York..	Welch........Boyle	10	4- 3
Aug. 29	" v. "	New York..	Keefe........Shreve	10	5- 4
May 23	Chicago v. Philadelph'a	Philadelp'a	Ryan......Buffinton	12	6- 5

DRAWN GAMES.

Date.	Contesting Clubs.	Cities.	Pitch'rs	Innings	Score.
July 19	Detroit v. Washington.	Washingt'n	Getzein........Shaw	10	2- 2
June 23	Philadelphia v. Chicago	Chicago....	Casey......Baldwin	13	7- 7
May 5	Boston v. New York...	New York.	Radbourne....Welch	10	6- 6

EAST VS. WEST.

THE LEAGUE TOURS OF 1887.

Each year sees the battle for supremacy between the representative professional teams of the East and the West increasing in interest. In 1886 the Western teams of the League's championship arena led the Eastern teams by a record of 145 victories to 132, Chicago and Detroit then tying for the leadership in the West in defeating Eastern teams, while New York took the lead of the Eastern teams in whipping Western opponents. In 1887, however, the tables were turned, the four Eastern League teams defeating the four Western by 147 victories to 136. Philadelphia led the Eastern teams in defeating Western opponents, and Detroit led the Western teams in whipping Eastern adversaries.

The East vs. West campaign of 1887 began with the visit of the Western teams to the East in the middle of May, the opening day being May 16, when the Indianapolis team played in New York; the Detroits in Philadelphia; the Pittsburgs at Boston, and the Chicagos at Washington. The tour lasted until June 1, when the Western teams returned home. On this tour the Western teams won but 21 victories to the Eastern teams' 31, as will be seen by the appended record:

THE FIRST TOUR EAST.

	Detroit.	Chicago.	Pittsburg.	Indianapolis.	Won.		Boston.	New York.	Washington.	Philadelphia.	Won.
Boston	2	2	3	3	10	Detroit	1	1	2	4	8
New York	2	1	3	3	9	Chicago	1	2	1	2	6
Philadelphia	0	2	2	3	7	Pittsburg	1	1	1	1	4
Washington	1	3	0	1	5	Indianapolis	1	1	1	0	3
Lost	5	8	8	10	31	Lost	4	5	5	7	21

Boston bore off the honors for the East, that team winning ten of three victories, Detroit doing the best for the West.

The Eastern teams began their first Western tour on June 21, when the Philadelphia team opened in Chicago, the Bostons in Indianapolis, and the Washingtons in Detroit, rain preventing the New York game in Pittsburgh. On this trip the Western teams offset their losses on their Eastern tour by winning 28 victories to the Eastern teams' 20, Chicago leading the West with ten victories, and New York the East with seven. Here is the record of the tour in full:

	Chicago.	Detroit.	Pittsburg.	Indianapolis.	Won.		New York.	Philadelphia.	Washington.	Boston.	Won.
New York	0	2	2	3	7	Chicago	3	2	2	3	10
Boston	1	0	3	1	5	Detroit	1	3	3	2	9
Philadelphia	0	1	0	3	4	Pittsburg	1	0	2	2	5
Washington	1	0	0	1	4	Indianapolis	0	1	1	2	4
Lost	2	3	5	8	20	Lost	5	6	8	9	28

This trip ended July 5, and on the 7th of July the Western teams began their second tour eastward, the Detroits opening at New York and the Chicagos at Philadelphia on that date. On this tour Chicago took the lead of the Western teams, while Philadelphia led the Eastern. Detroit made a very poor show on this tour, they winning but three games out of eleven, while Chicago won seven out of twelve. But Philadelphia bore off the palm in winning ten out of fifteen, though they lost three straight with Chicago. They offset this by defeating Detroit three straight. New York showed up the weakest against the Western teams on this trip, they only winning single games from Detroit, Chicago and Pittsburg. Here is the full record of the trip, which ended July 22, the East winning by 30 to 19:

	Chicago.	Indianapolis.	Detroit.	Pittsburg.	Won.		Boston.	Philadelphia.	Washington.	New York.	Won.
Philadelphia..	0	3	3	4	10	Chicago......	1	3	1	2	7
Washington .	2	1	2	3	8	Pittsburg	0	2	1	2	5
Boston...	2	1	2	1	6	Indianapolis .	1	0	3	0	4
New York ..	1	3	1	1	6	Detroit.....	1	0	0	2	3
Lost........	5	8	8	9	30	Lost ...	3	5	5	6	19

The Eastern teams began their second tour West on July 28, when New York opened at Detroit, and Boston at Chicago. On this trip Philadelphia led the Eastern teams, and they returned the compliment Chicago paid them earlier in the month by whipping the champions three games at Chicago. The Western teams had the best of it, however, by a record of twenty-four victories, to the East's twenty-three. Here is the record, the tour ending August 6:

	Detroit.	Chicago.	Indianapolis.	Pittsburg.	Won.		Philadelphia.	Washington.	New York.	Boston.	Won.
Philadelphia.	1	3	2	2	8	Detroit......	2	2	2	2	8
New York...	1	1	2	2	6	Chicago......	1	3	2	2	8
Boston........	2	1	2	0	5	Pittsburg	2	0	1	3	6
Washington .	1	0	0	3	4	Indianapolis..	0	0	1	1	2
Lost	5	5	6	7	23	Lost	5	5	6	8	24

The third trip of the Western teams East began August 8, when the Chicago champions opened at New York, and the

Detroits at Boston. On this tour Detroit rallied finely, winning nine out of eleven games, while Chicago fell off, they losing five out of nine. It was a close struggle in the aggregate, as the East won twenty-one games to the West's twenty. The trip ended on September 3. The record in full is appended:

	Detroit.	Pittsburg.	Chicago.	Indianapolis.	Won.		Boston.	Philadelphia.	New York.	Washington.	Won.
Philadelphia.	1	1	1	3	6	Detroit.......	3	1	2	3	9
New York...	1	1	2	2	6	Pittsburg	0	2	1	2	5
Boston.......	0	2	0	3	5	Chicago......	0	1	2	1	4
Washington.	0	1	1	2	4	Indianapolis.	0	0	0	2	2
Lost.......	2	5	4	10	21	Lost.......	3	4	5	8	20

The third trip of the Eastern teams Westward, began September 12, when the Philadelphias played at Chicago, and the Bostons at Detroit. The champions took the Phillies into camp, easily winning three straight, but Philadelphia led the East on the tour, Chicago doing the best for the West, with nine victories out of eleven games. The record of the trip which ended Sept. 24, resulted in the success of the West by 24 to 22, as follows:

	Chicago.	Detroit.	Pittsburg.	Indianapolis.	Won.		Philadelphia.	New York.	Boston.	Washington.	Won.
Philadelphia.	0	2	3	3	8	Chicago......	3	1	2	3	9
New York...	1	1	3	2	7	Detroit.......	0	2	2	3	7
Boston	0	1	2	1	4	Pittsburg	0	0	1	3	4
Washington..	0	0	0	3	3	Indianapolis.	0	1	2	1	4
Lost.......	1	4	8	9	22	Lost.......	3	4	7	10	24

The Record in full for 1887 is as follows:

EASTERN VICTORIES.						WESTERN VICTORIES.					
	Detroit.	Chicago.	Pittsburg.	Indianapolis.	Won.		Philadelphia.	New York.	Boston.	Washington.	Won.
Philadelphia.	8	6	12	17	43	Detroit	10	10	11	13	44
New York...	8	6	12	15	41	Chicago......	12	11	9	11	43
Boston.......	7	6	11	11	35	Pittsburg.....	6	6	7	9	28
Washington.	4	7	9	8	28	Indianapolis.	1	3	7	10	21
Lost.......	27	25	44	51	147	Lost.......	29	30	34	43	136

HOME AND HOME GAMES.

The Record of the Home and Home Games of the campaign of 1887 is appended:

EASTERN CLUBS.	Philadelphia.	New York.	Boston.	Washington.	Won.	WESTERN CLUBS.	Detroit.	Chicago.	Pittsburg.	Indianapolis.	Won.
Philadelphia.	....	10	9	13	32	Detroit........	....	8	13	14	35
New York...	7	....	10	10	27	Chicago......	10	....	5	13	28
Boston.......	9	7	....	10	26	Pittsburg.....	4	12	....	11	27
Washington.	3	8	7	....	18	Indianapolis.	4	5	7	....	16
Lost.......	19	25	26	33	103	Lost........	18	25	25	38	106

THE CHAMPIONSHIP RECORDS.

THE FIRST PROFESSIONAL ASSOCIATION.

THE OLD NATIONAL ASSOCIATION.

The baseball fraternity of the country, up to 1857, were without any governing organization to provide authorized rules of play for the game. In 1857, however, the first National Association sprang into existence, and it gave laws to the ball players of the country, up to 1870, by which time so greatly had the game spread in popularity, that the opportunity for the introduction of professional exemplars of the game was presented. In fact, some professionalism had prevailed to a more or less extent for some years prior to that; but up to 1870 but one National Association existed in the entire country, and the last convention held by that organization occurred in that year. In 1871 Mr. Chadwick divided the clubs into two classes, and he organized the first regular professional association in that year, the convention which he called, assembling at Collier's Saloon—the well known actor—on the corner of Broadway and Thirteenth Street, New York, on the night of March 17, 1871. At that convention the first special code of championship rules ever put in operation were adopted, and in that year the first officially recognized championship contests known in the history of the game were played. The season began in May with the Athletic, Boston, Chicago, Cleveland, Forest City Club, Haymakers of Troy, Mutual, Olympic, of Washington, Kekionga and Rockford, Forest City Clubs, in the arena. The Eckfords entered in August, but their games were not counted. The Kekionga games were thrown out owing to illegal games after July. The record which decided the championship of 1871 was as follows:

RECORD FOR 1871.

CLUB.	Athletic.	Boston.	Chicago.	Mutual.	Olympic.	Haymaker.	Cleveland.	Kekionga.	Rockford.	Games Won.
Athletic........................	....	1	3	3	3	3	3	3	3	22
Boston..........................	3	....	1	3	3	3	3	3	3	22
Chicago........................	2	3	....	3	3	1	2	3	3	20
Mutual..........................	2	2	1	....	3	1	2	3	3	17
Olympic........................	0	1	2	1	....	3	3	3	3	16
Haymaker......................	0	2	1	3	2	....	2	3	2	15
Cleveland......................	0	1	1	3	0	2	....	0	3	10
Kekionga.......................	0	0	0	1	1	1	3	....	1	7
Rockford.......................	0	0	0	1	0	1	1	3	....	6
Games Lost...................	7	10	9	18	15	15	19	21	21	135

In 1872 the Baltimores entered the list, as also the Atlantics of Brooklyn, and the Troy Club, and Washington sent two clubs, both of which failed, however; the brunt of the battle that year lying between the five clubs of Boston, Baltimore, New York, Philadelphia and Troy. The result of the pennant race of 1872 was as follows:

RECORD FOR 1872.

CLUB.	Boston.	Baltimore.	Mutual.	Athletic.	Troy.	Atlantic.	Cleveland.	Mansfield.	Eckford.	Olympic.	National.	Games Won.
Boston............	....	7	7	4	2	7	4	3	3	1	1	39
Baltimore........	0	....	5	4	3	4	4	4	5	2	3	34
Mutual............	2	4	....	6	3	6	2	4	5	1	1	34
Athletic..........	4	5	3	....	2	4	3	2	5	1	1	30
Troy..............	1	0	2	0	....	2	1	4	3	1	1	15
Atlantic..........	1	1	2	0	0	....	0	2	2	0	0	8
Cleveland.......	0	1	1	0	0	1	....	0	1	1	1	6
Mansfield.......	0	0	0	0	0	1	1	....	2	0	1	5
Eckford..........	0	1	0	0	0	2	0	0	....	0	0	3
Olympic.........	0	0	0	0	0	0	0	0	0	....	2	2
National.........	0	0	0	0	0	0	0	0	0	0	....	0
Games Lost.....	8	19	20	14	10	27	15	19	26	7	11	176

In 1873 the Athletics had a local rival team to meet in the championship arena, in the new Philadelphia Club, which, but for crookedness in its ranks, would have won the championship that year. Baltimore also sent two clubs, and Elizabeth, N. J. entered the list. The record for 1873 was as follows:

RECORD FOR 1873.

CLUB.	Boston	Philadelphia	Baltimore	Mutual	Athletic	Atlantic	Washington	Resolute	Maryland	Games Won
Boston...........	....	5	7	6	4	8	9	4	0	43
Philadelphia.....	4	....	6	4	8	7	3	4	0	36
Baltimore........	2	3	....	6	3	7	6	3	3	33
Mutual...........	3	4	3	....	4	7	4	4	0	29
Athletic..........	5	1	4	5	....	5	6	2	0	28
Atlantic..........	1	2	2	2	4	....	3	3	0	17
Washington......	0	2	0	1	0	2	....	1	2	8
Resolute.........	1	0	0	0	0	1	0	....	0	2
Maryland.........	0	0	0	0	0	0	0	0	....	0
Games Lost......	16	17	22	24	23	37	31	21	5	196

In 1874 Hartford sent a club to compete for the pennant. The Olympic, Kekionga, Rockford, Eckford, Mansfield, Maryland, and Haymakers having retired since 1871 and up to 1873, inclusive, the Chicago Club, which had been broken up by the great fire of October, 1871, and had been out of the race in 1872 and 1873, again entered the lists. At the end of the season the record stood as follows:

RECORD FOR 1874.

CLUB.	Boston	Mutual	Athletic	Philadelphia	Chicago	Atlantic	Hartford	Baltimore	Games Won
Boston...........	....	5	8	8	7	6	9	9	52
Mutual...........	5	....	4	1	9	7	8	8	42
Athletic..........	2	6	....	9	3	6	5	2	33
Philadelphia.....	2	5	1	....	7	6	4	4	29
Chicago..........	3	1	4	3	....	4	4	9	27
Atlantic..........	4	3	1	3	3	....	5	3	23
Hartford.........	1	2	3	4	1	3	....	3	17
Baltimore........	1	1	2	1	1	1	2	....	9
Games Lost......	18	23	23	29	31	33	37	38	232

The season of 1875 saw the last of the old National professional Association, it being superseded by the League in 1876. In 1875 St. Louis entered the lists and before the season expired there were thirteen competitors in the arena, and things became decidedly mixed, and demoralization set in. The outcome of the contest, however, was the success of the Boston Club, which had won the championship each successive season since 1871.

The record of the last season's campaign of the old National Association which closed its season in 1875, was as follows.

RECORD FOR 1875.

CLUB.	Boston.	Athletic.	Hartford.	St. Louis.	Philadelphia.	Chicago.	Mutual.	New Haven	Red Stock'gs	Washington.	Centennial.	Atlantic.	Western.	Games Won.
Boston........	...	8	9	7	6	8	10	5	1	5	5	6	1	71
Athletic............	2	...	3	6	8	7	6	7	0	5	2	7	0	53
Hartford....	1	4	...	5	4	6	8	8	3	4	1	10	0	54
St. Louis...........	2	1	5	...	5	5	8	2	2	3	0	2	4	39
Philadelphia.....	0	2	4	5	...	7	2	4	1	2	3	7	0	37
Chicago..............	2	1	4	5	3	...	3	2	4	0	0	2	4	30
Mutual.....	0	3	2	0	5	3	...	4	2	0	2	7	1	29
New Haven..........	1	0	1	1	0	1	1	...	0	1	0	1	0	7
Red Stockings........	0	0	0	0	0	0	0	0	...	2	0	0	2	4
Washington....	0	0	0	0	0	0	0	4	0	...	0	0	0	4
Centennial.............	0	1	0	0	0	0	0	1	0	0	...	0	0	2
Atlantic....	0	0	0	0	0	0	2	0	0	0	0	...	0	2
Western....	0	0	0	0	0	0	0	0	1	0	0	0	...	1
Games Lost..........	8	20	28	29	31	37	38	39	14	22	13	42	12	333

THE LEAGUE CHAMPIONSHIP RECORD.

FROM 1876 TO 1887, INCLUSIVE.

The organization of the National League in 1876 began a new era in the history of professional ball playing. Prior to this year the first professional National Association had ruled the fraternity from 1871 to 1875 under circumstances which had proved to be anything but advantageous to their welfare; and by 1876 the existing condition of things had become such as to render a reform movement essential to the permanent existence of the best clubs of the Association; and consequently in 1876 a division in the ranks of the Association occurred, and the National League took the place as the ruling power of the professional clubs of the old National Professional Association, and from 1876 until 1882 the League stood alone at the head of the fraternity as the governing professional organization of the country. In 1882 the American Association was established, and from that year to the close of 1887 it grew to be a powerful rival of the League and finally it joined forces with the senior organization under the protective power of the National agreement.

In the inaugural year of the League eight clubs entered the lists for championship, the clubs represented being Boston, Hartford, New York and Philadelphia in the East, and Chicago, Cincinnati, Louisville and St. Louis in the West. The record for that year gave the championship to the Chicago Club, as will be seen by the appended table:

RECORD FOR 1876.

CLUB.	Chicago.	Hartford.	St. Louis.	Boston.	Louisville.	Mutual.	Athletic.	Cincinnati.	Games Play'd	Games Lost.	Games Won.
Chicago.........	....	6	4	9	9	7	7	10	66	14	52
Hartford.........	4	....	4	8	9	4	9	9	68	21	47
St. Louis.........	6	6	....	6	6	6	8	7	64	19	45
Boston...........	1	2	4	....	5	8	9	10	70	31	39
Louisville.......	1	1	4	5	....	5	6	8	66	36	30
Mutual..........	1	4	1	2	3	....	3	7	56	35	21
Athletic.........	1	1	0	1	2	4	....	5	59	45	14
Cincinnati.......	0	1	2	0	2	1	3	....	65	56	9
Games Lost......	14	21	19	31	36	35	45	56	514	257	257

In 1877 the Mutual Club of New York and the Athletic of Philadelphia were not among the contestants, owing to their failure to fulfill their scheduled engagements of the previous season, and consequently only five clubs, of the eight which entered the lists in 1876, took part in the championship campaign of 1877. This year Boston went to the front again while Chicago had to be content with the rear rank position, as will be seen from the appended record:

THE RECORD FOR 1877.

CLUB.	Boston.	Louisville.	Hartford.	St. Louis.	Chicago.	Games Play'd	Games Lost.	Games Won.
Boston...........	....	8	7	6	10	48	17	31
Louisville.......	4	....	6	10	8	48	20	28
Hartford.........	5	6	....	5	8	48	24	24
St. Louis.........	6	2	4	....	4	48	29	19
Chicago..........	2	4	7	8	..	48	30	18
Games Lost......	17	20	24	29	30		120	120

In 1878 only six clubs took part in the season's campaign as in 1877; but Providence took the place of Hartford, Indianapolis filled Louisville's place, and Milwaukee that of St. Louis.

Once more the championship honors were held by Boston, while Chicago pulled up to a better position than they held in 1877, as the appended record shows:

THE RECORD FOR 1878.

CLUB.	Boston.	Cincinnati.	Providence.	Chicago.	Indianapolis.	Milwaukee.	Games Play'd	Games Lost.	Games Won.
Boston..................	....	6	6	8	10	11	60	19	41
Cincinnati..............	6	....	9	10	4	8	60	23	37
Providence.............	6	3	....	6	10	8	60	27	33
Chicago................	4	2	6	....	8	10	60	30	30
Indianapolis...........	2	8	2	4	....	8	60	36	24
Milwaukee.............	1	4	4	2	4	....	60	45	15
Games Lost............	19	23	27	30	36	45	360	180	180

In 1879 eight clubs once more entered the lists for the League championship, and this number was finally fixed upon as the maximum of membership of the National League. In the place of Indianapolis and Milwaukee, Buffalo and Cleveland entered the race, while two new members were taken in from Syracuse and Troy. It was in this year that George Wright left the Boston Club and became the manager of the rival club of that city from Providence, and he signalized the event by winning the pennant from Boston for the Providence Club, the Stars of Syracuse being distanced in the pennant race, while Troy made a very poor show, as the record below proves.

THE RECORD FOR 1879.

CLUB.	Providence.	Boston.	Chicago.	Buffalo.	Cincinnati.	Cleveland.	Troy City.	Syracuse.	Games Play'd	Games Lost.	Games Won.
Providence.............	....	8	7	6	10	8	10	6	78	23	55
Boston.................	4	....	4	9	7	10	11	4	78	29	49
Chicago................	5	8	....	6	3	8	8	6	76	32	44
Buffalo................	6	3	6	....	7	8	11	3	76	32	44
Cincinnati.............	2	5	8	3	....	8	9	3	74	36	38
Cleveland..............	4	2	4	4	4	....	5	1	77	53	24
Troy City..............	2	1	3	1	2	6	....	4	75	56	19
Syracuse...............	0	2	0	3	3	5	2	....	42	27	15
Games Lost............	23	29	32	32	36	53	56	27		288	288

In 1880 eight clubs again entered the arena, Worcester taking the place of the disbanded Syracuse Stars, which club found their League adversaries altogether too strong for them. This year Chicago went to the front again, Cincinnati falling off so badly in the race that at the finish they were found to be badly distanced, as the record below shows:

THE RECORD FOR 1880.

CLUB.	Chicago.	Providence.	Cleveland.	Troy City.	Worcester.	Boston.	Buffalo.	Cincinnati.	Games Play'd	Games Lost.	Games Won.
Chicago...........	....	9	8	10	10	9	11	10	84	17	67
Providence.........	3	....	9	7	6	7	10	10	84	32	52
Cleveland.........	4	3	....	9	6	7	9	9	84	37	47
Troy City.........	2	5	3	....	5	8	11	10	83	42	41
Worcester.........	2	6	6	7	....	8	3	8	83	43	40
Boston.............	3	5	5	7	4	....	9	7	84	44	40
Buffalo.............	1	2	3	1	9	3	....	5	82	58	24
Cincinnati.........	2	2	3	1	3	5	5	....	80	59	21
Games Lost.......	17	32	37	42	43	44	58	59		332	312

In 1881 no change was made in the League ranks, and the same cities were represented in the pennant race of that year as in 1880. Once more the Chicago Club bore off the season's honors, that club having learned the value of team-work as a potent factor in winning the League championship honors. This year Worcester, which club made so good a fight in 1880, fell off to last place, and Boston also occupied an inferior position in the year's campaign, their falling off during 1880 and 1881 being a feature of the year's events. Then, too, Cincinnati was forced to tender its resignation and Detroit was given that club's place, and the new club made a very good showing in the campaign of '81, as will be seen by the appended record:

THE RECORD FOR 1881.

CLUB.	Chicago.	Providence.	Buffalo.	Detroit.	Troy City.	Boston.	Cleveland.	Worcester.	Games Play'd	Games Lost.	Games Won.
Chicago...........	....	9	7	7	8	10	6	9	84	28	56
Providence.........	3	....	5	8	6	7	9	9	84	37	47
Buffalo.............	5	7	....	9	3	8	7	6	83	38	45
Detroit.............	5	4	3	....	7	8	7	7	84	43	41
Troy City.........	4	6	9	5	....	5	6	4	84	45	39
Boston.............	2	5	4	4	7	....	8	8	83	45	38
Cleveland.........	6	3	5	5	6	4	....	7	84	48	36
Worcester.........	3	3	5	5	8	3	5	....	82	50	32
Games Lost.......	28	37	38	43	45	45	48	50		334	334

In 1882 the same eight clubs again entered the lists, and for the third time in succession Chicago carried off the championship, with Providence a close second again as they were in '81 and '80. Worcester was again badly distanced, and as a penalty the club was retired at the close of the season. The Troy club, too, did not show up well this year, and they, too, shared the fate of the Worcesters. The record at the close stood as follows:

THE RECORD FOR 1882.

CLUB.	Chicago.	Providence.	Buffalo.	Boston.	Cleveland.	Detroit.	Troy City.	Worcester.	Games Play'd	Games Lost.	Games Won.
Chicago.............	....	8	6	6	9	8	9	9	84	29	55
Providence...........	4	....	6	6	8	9	9	10	84	32	52
Buffalo..............	6	6	....	5	6	8	6	11	84	39	45
Boston..............	6	6	7	....	7	8	4	7	84	39	45
Cleveland...........	3	4	6	5	....	4	9	11	82	40	42
Detroit.............	4	3	7	4	7	....	8	9	83	41	42
Troy City...........	3	3	6	8	2	4	....	9	83	48	35
Worcester...........	3	2	1	5	1	3	3	....	84	66	18
Games Lost.........	29	32	39	39	40	41	48	66		334	334

In 1883 New York and Philadelphia were elected as League cities in the place of Troy and Worcester, and this time the Boston Club, by a plucky rally toward the close of the season, managed to get in front of Chicago, the latter club being obliged to be content with second place. Neither New York nor Philadelphia made much of a show in the campaign, both of them occupying rear positions, as will be seen by the appended record:

THE RECORD FOR 1883.

CLUB.	Boston.	Chicago.	Providence.	Cleveland.	Buffalo.	New York.	Detroit.	Philadelphia.	Games Play'd	Games Lost.	Games Won.
Boston..............	....	7	8	10	7	7	10	14	98	35	63
Chicago.............	7	....	7	6	9	9	9	12	98	39	59
Providence..........	6	7	....	6	7	9	12	11	98	40	58
Cleveland...........	4	8	8	....	7	7	9	12	97	42	55
Buffalo.............	7	5	7	7	....	8	9	9	97	45	52
New York...........	7	5	5	6	5	....	6	12	96	50	46
Detroit.............	4	5	2	5	5	8	....	11	98	58	40
Philadelphia........	0	2	3	2	5	2	3	....	98	81	17
Games Lost.........	35	39	40	42	45	50	58	81		390	390

In 1884 the same eight clubs again entered the lists, and this time the Providence Club took the lead of both Boston and Chicago, and came in victors after the most brilliant campaign known in the history of the club, the team toward the close working together as a whole in model style. New York and Philadelphia improved upon their previous season's record, but failed to reach the position in the race they had expected. Cleveland fell off badly in the race, and finally resigned its membership early in the ensuing year. The record for 1884 is as follows:

THE RECORD FOR 1884.

CLUB.	Providence.	Boston.	Buffalo.	Chicago.	New York.	Philadelphia.	Cleveland.	Detroit.	Games Play'd	Games Lost.	Games Won.
Providence	....	9	10	11	13	13	13	15	112	28	84
Boston	7	....	9	10	8	13	14	12	111	38	73
Buffalo	6	6	....	10	5	11	14	12	111	47	64
Chicago	5	6	6	....	12	14	8	11	112	50	62
New York	3	8	11	4	....	11	11	14	112	50	62
Philadelphia	3	3	5	2	5	.	10	11	112	73	39
Cleveland	3	2	2	8	5	6	..1.	9	112	77	35
Detroit	1	4	4	5	2	5	7	....	112	84	28
Games Lost	28	38	47	50	50	73	77	84		447	447

In 1885 Cleveland retired from the League, and St. Louis was elected to fill the vacancy, and again eight clubs entered the lists. In the pennant race both New York and Philadelphia improved upon their work in 1884, the former team giving the Chicago team a very close push for the goal, Philadelphia coming in a good third. The full record of the season in the championship arena is as follows:

THE RECORD FOR 1885.

CLUB.	Chicago.	New York.	Philadelphia.	Providence.	Boston.	Detroit.	Buffalo.	St. Louis.	Games Play'd	Games Lost.	Games Won.
Chicago	....	6	11	11	14	15	16	14	112	25	87
New York	10	....	11	12	13	12	15	12	112	27	85
Philadelphia	5	5	....	8	9	9	11	9	110	54	56
Providence	5	4	7	....	7	9	13	8	110	57	53
Boston	2	3	7	9	....	7	10	8	108	66	46
Detroit	1	4	7	6	9	....	5	9	108	67	41
Buffalo	0	1	5	3	6	11	....	12	110	74	38
St. Louis	2	4	6	8	8	4	4	....	108	72	36
Games Lost	25	27	54	57	66	67	74	72		442	442

BASE BALL GUIDE.

In 1886 Providence and Buffalo were retired from the League, Kansas City and Washington taking their places. In the pennant race, while Chicago again took the lead, Detroit pushed New York back to third place, and Philadelphia had to be content with fourth position. The record in full is appended:

THE RECORD FOR 1886.

CLUB.	Chicago.	Detroit.	New York.	Philadelphia.	Boston.	St. Louis.	Kansas City.	Washington.	Games Play'd	Games Won.	Games Lost.
Chicago............	....	11	10	10	12	13	17	17	124	90	34
Detroit............	7	....	11	10	11	15	16	17	123	87	36
New York..........	8	7	....	8	11	15	15	11	119	75	44
Philadelphia.......	7	7	8	....	10	12	14	13	114	71	43
Boston............	6	6	6	3	....	11	11	13	117	56	61
St. Louis..........	4	2	3	6	6	....	12	10	122	43	79
Kansas City.......	1	2	3	2	6	5	....	11	121	30	91
Washington.......	1	1	3	4	5	8	6	....	120	28	92
Games Lost.......	34	36	44	43	61	79	91	92		480	480

In 1887 Pittsburg left the American Association and joined the League, replacing the St. Louis League Club, while the Indianapolis Club was given the Kansas City franchise. In the pennant race Detroit took the lead, Philadelphia being second, while the Chicago champions this year had to be content with third position. The record in full is as follows:

THE RECORD FOR 1887.

CLUB.	Detroit.	Philadelphia.	Chicago.	New York.	Boston.	Pittsburg.	Washington.	Indianapolis.	Games Play'd	Games Won.	Games Lost.
Detroit............	....	10	8	10	11	13	13	14	124	79	45
Philadelphia......	8	....	6	10	9	12	13	17	123	75	48
Chicago...........	10	12	....	11	9	5	11	13	121	71	50
New York.........	8	7	6	....	10	12	10	15	123	68	55
Boston............	7	9	6	7	....	11	10	11	121	61	60
Pittsburg..........	4	6	12	6	7	....	9	11	124	55	69
Washington.......	4	3	7	8	7	9	....	8	120	46	76
Indianapolis.......	4	1	5	3	7	7	10	....	126	37	89
Games Lost.......	45	48	50	55	60	69	76	89		492	492

Before the organization of the first Professional National Association, there was no recognized code of rules governing any championship contest in the base ball arena, only a nominal title existing prior to 1871, and even that was frequently disputed. The original champions of the old amateur class of clubs, which existed at the home of base ball, in New York and its suburbs, was the Atlantic Club, of Brooklyn, the champion team of that club, when it was in its palmiest amateur days, being M. O'Brien, pitcher; Boerum, catcher; Price, John Oliver and Charlie Smith on the bases; Dick Pearce, short stop, and P. O'Brien, Archy McMahon and Tice Hamilton in the outfield. This was in 1860, when they won the championship from the Excelsiors. When they defeated the Mutuals and Eckfords, in 1864, their champion team was Pratt, pitcher; Ferguson, catcher; Start, Crane and Smith on the bases; Pearce, at shortfield, and Chapman, Joe Oliver and Sid Smith in the outfield. The Eckfords held the nominal title in 1862 and '63, and in 1869 the Cincinnati Red Stockings were indisputably the champions of the United States. Their team in that year included Asa Brainard, as pitcher; D. Allison, as catcher; Gould Sweazy and Waterman, on the bases; George Wright, as short stop, and Leonard, Harry Wright and McVey in the outfield. In 1870 the title was claimed by the Mutuals and Chicagos, and the disputed claim was never settled.

In 1871 the Professional National Association was organized, and then was begun the first series of championship matches under an official code of rules known in the history of professional ball playing. From this year to 1876, when the National League was organized, the winning teams were as follows:

1871, Athletic—McBride, pitcher; Malone, catcher; Fisler, Reach and Meyerle, on the bases; Radcliff, short stop; Cuthbert, Sensenderfer and Heubel, in the outfield.

1872, Boston—A. G. Spalding, pitcher; C. A. McVey, catcher; Chas. Gould, Ross Barnes and Harry Schafer, on the bases; Geo. Wright, short stop; Andy Leonard, Harry Wright and Fraley Rogers in the outfield.

1873, Boston—A. G. Spalding, pitcher; Jas. White, catcher; James O'Rourke, Barnes and Schafer, on the bases; Geo. Wright, short stop; Leonard, Harry Wright and Manning, in the outfield.

1874, Boston—A. G. Spalding, pitcher; McVey, catcher; Jas. White, Barnes and Schafer, on the bases; Geo. Wright, short stop; Leonard, Hall and Jas. O'Rourke, in the outfield.

1875, Boston—A. G. Spalding, pitcher; James White, catcher; Latham, Barnes and Schafer, on the bases; George Wright, short stop; Leonard, Jas. O'Rourke and Manning, in the outfield,

From 1876 to 1887, inclusive, the winning teams in the League arena were as follows:

1876 Chicago—A. G. Spalding, pitcher; Jas. White, catcher; McVey, Barnes and Anson, on the bases; Peters, short stop; Glenn, Hines and Addy, in the outfield.

1877, Boston—Bond, pitcher; Brown, catcher; Jas. White, Geo. Wright and Morrill, on the bases; Sutton, short stop; Leonard, Jas. O'Rourke and Schafer, in the outfield.

1878, Boston—Bond, pitcher; Snyder, catcher; Morrill, Burdock and Sutton, on the bases; Geo. Wright, short stop; Leonard, Jas. O'Rourke and Manning in the outfield.

1879, Providence—Ward, pitcher; Brown, catcher; Start, McGeary and Hague, on the bases; Geo. Wright, short stop; York, Hines and Jas. O'Rourke, in the outfield.

1880, 1881 and 1882, Chicago—Corcoran and Goldsmith, pitchers; Flint, catcher; Anson, Quest and Williamson, on the bases; Burns, short stop; Dalrymple, Gore and Kelly, in the outfield.

1883, Boston—Whitney and Buffinton, pitchers; Hines and Hackett, catchers; Morrill, Burdock and Sutton, on the bases; Wise, short stop, and Hornung, Smith and Radford, in the outfield.

1884, Providence—Radbourne, pitcher; Gilligan and Nava catchers; Start, Farrell and Denny, on the bases; Irwin, short stop, and Carroll, Hines and Radford in the outfield.

1885, Chicago—Clarkson and McCormick, pitchers; Flint, catcher; Anson, Pfeffer and Williamson, on the bases; Burns, short stop, and Dalrymple, Gore and Kelly, in the outfield.

1886, Chicago—Clarkson, McCormick and Flynn, pitchers; Kelly and Flint, catchers; Anson, Pfeffer and Burns on the bases; Williamson, short stop, and Dalrymple, Gore, Kelly, Ryan and Sunday in the outfield.

1887, Detroit—Getzein, Baldwin, Conway, Twitchell and Weidman, pitchers; Bennett, Briody and Ganzel, catchers; Brouthers, Dunlap and White, on the bases; Rowe, short stop, and Richardson, Dunlap and Thompson in the outfield.

EAST VS. WEST.

THE LEAGUE CONTESTS FOR TEN YEARS.

The following is the record of the contests between the Eastern and Western Clubs of the League from its organization in 1876, to the close of the first decade of its history in 1886.

THE RECORD OF 1876.

Eight clubs entered the lists in 1876, and the West won by the score of 77 victories to the East's 66, as follows:

	Hartford	Mutual	Boston	Athletic	Won		Chicago	St. Louis	Louisville	Cincinnati	Won
Chicago......	6	7	9	7	29	Hartford....	4	4	9	9	26
St. Louis	6	6	6	8	26	Boston	1	4	5	10	20
Louisville....	1	5	5	6	17	Mutual.......	1	1	3	7	12
Cincinnati...	1	1	0	3	5	Athletic . .	1	0	2	5	8
Lost.........	14	19	20	24	77	Lost..... .	7	9	19	31	66

THE RECORD OF 1877.

In 1877 six clubs entered the pennant race, but only four completed their schedule of games, the Cincinnati club's games being thrown out of the count. The full record gave the East 61 victories to the West's 33, but the legal count lessened these figures to 43 for the East against 29 for the West, as will be seen by the appended table. As two Eastern clubs played against four Western teams, the victory is quite noteworthy. The record is as follows:

	St. Louis	Louisville	Chicago	Won		Boston	Hartford	Won
Boston...........	6	8	10	24	St. Louis.........	6	4	10
Hartford..........	5	6	8	19	Louisville..........	4	6	10
					Chicago..........	2	7	9
Lost.............	11	14	18	43	Lost.............	12	17	29

THE RECORD OF 1878.

In 1878 six clubs again entered the race and the two from the East again defeated the four from the West by 62 victories to 34, another signal mark of superiority for the Eastern teams. The record is as follows:

	Cincinnati	Chicago	Milwaukee	Indianapolis	Won		Boston	Providence	Won
Boston	6	8	11	10	35	Cincinnati............	6	9	15
Providence...	3	6	8	10	27	Chicago	4	6	10
						Milwaukee............	1	4	5
						Indianapolis	2	2	4
Lost........	9	14	19	20	62	Lost	13	21	34

THE RECORD OF 1879.

In 1879 eight clubs began to be the regular number of contestants in the League arena, and they have been kept at that number ever since. In this year the East once more went to the front, but the contest proved to be a close one, as the Eastern clubs only won the lead by 84 victories to 81, as will be seen by the appended record :

	Chicago.	Buffalo.	Cincinnati.	Cleveland.	Won.		Syracuse.	Providence.	Boston.	Troy.	Won.
Providence...	7	6	10	8	31	Chicago......	6	5	8	8	27
Boston.......	4	9	7	10	30	Buffalo	3	6	3	11	23
Troy.........	3	1	2	6	12	Cincinnati ...	3	2	5	9	19
Syracuse.....	0	3	3	5	11	Cleveland.....	1	4	2	5	12
Lost	14	19	22	29	84	Lost........	13	17	28	33	81

THE RECORD OF 1880.

In 1880 the East for the fourth successive season bore off the palm by a record of 101 victories to 89, as follows :

	Chicago.	Cleveland.	Buffalo.	Cincinnati.	Won.		Providence.	Troy.	Boston.	Worcester.	Won.
Providence...	3	9	10	10	32	Chicago......	9	10	9	10	38
Troy.........	2	3	11	10	26	Cleveland	3	9	7	6	25
Boston.......	3	5	9	7	24	Buffalo.......	2	1	3	9	15
Worcester....	2	6	3	8	19	Cincinnati....	2	1	5	3	11
Lost........	10	23	33	35	101	Lost	16	21	24	28	89

THE RECORD OF 1881.

In 1881 the West began to take the lead, they winning this year by a record of 106 victories to 85, as follows:

	Providence.	Troy.	Worcester.	Boston.	Won.		Chicago.	Detroit.	Buffalo.	Cleveland.	Won.
Chicago......	9	8	9	10	36	Providence.	3	8	5	9	25
Detroit.......	4	7	7	8	26	Troy.	4	5	9	6	24
Buffalo.......	7	3	6	8	24	Worcester.	3	5	5	5	18
Cleveland....	3	6	7	4	20	Boston.	2	4	4	8	18
Lost	23	24	29	30	106	Lost	12	22	23	28	85

THE RECORD OF 1882.

In 1882 the Western clubs made their best record of the ten years, they winning by 113 victories to 78, as follows:

	Boston.	Providence.	Troy.	Worcester.	Won.		Chicago.	Cleveland.	Buffalo.	Detroit.	Won.
Chicago	6	8	9	9	32	Boston	6	7	7	8	28
Cleveland	5	4	9	11	29	Providence	4	8	6	9	27
Buffalo	5	6	6	11	28	Troy	3	2	6	4	15
Detroit	4	3	8	9	24	Worcester	3	1	1	3	8
Lost	20	21	32	40	113	Lost	16	18	20	24	78

THE RECORD OF 1883.

In 1883 the West went to the front for the last time in the first decade of the League's history when they took the lead by 122 victories to 100, as follows:

	Boston.	Providence.	New York.	Philadelphia.	Won.		Chicago.	Cleveland.	Buffalo.	Detroit.	Won.
Chicago	7	7	9	12	35	Boston	7	10	7	10	34
Cleveland	4	8	7	12	31	Providence	7	6	7	12	32
Buffalo	7	7	8	9	31	New York	5	6	6	5	22
Detroit	4	2	8	11	25	Philadelphia	2	2	5	3	12
Lost	22	24	32	44	122	Lost	21	24	24	31	100

THE RECORD OF 1884.

In 1884 the Eastern Clubs again resumed their old time lead, and they claim that they went to the front to stay. In this year the East won by 162 victories to 93, then the best record, as follows:

BASE BALL GUIDE.   45

THE RECORD OF 1885.

In 1885 the East again took the lead, this time by 145 victories to 109, as follows:

	Chicago.	Detroit.	St. Louis.	Buffalo.	Won.		New York.	Providence.	Philadelphia.	Boston.	Won.
New York...	10	12	12	15	49	Chicago......	6	11	11	14	42
Providence...	5	9	8	13	35	Detroit.......	4	6	7	9	26
Philadelphia.	5	9	9	11	34	St. Louis.....	4	8	6	8	26
Boston.......	2	7	8	10	27	Buffalo.......	1	3	5	6	15
Lost........	22	37	37	49	145	Lost........	15	28	29	37	109

In 1886 the West went to the front again by a record of 145 victories to 132, as follows:

	New York.	Philadelphia.	Boston.	Washington.	Won.		Detroit.	Chicago.	Kansas City.	St. Louis.	Won.
Chicago.......	10	10	12	17	49	New York...	7	8	15	15	45
Detroit........	11	10	11	17	49	Philadelphia.	7	7	12	14	40
St. Louis.....	3	6	6	10	25	Boston.......	6	6	11	11	34
Kansas City..	3	2	6	11	22	Washington .	1	1	3	8	13
Lost4......	27	28	35	55	145	Lost........	21	22	41	48	132

The clubs which led in their respective sections each season were as follows: Chicago and Hartford in 1876; Boston and St. Louis in 1877; Boston and Cincinnati in 1878; Providence and Chicago in 1879 and also in 1880 and 1881; Chicago and Boston in 1882 and 1883; Providence and Chicago in 1884; New York and Chicago in 1885; Chicago and New York in 1886. By the above it will be seen that Chicago has occupied first or second place in the League race nine times during the eleven years' existence of the League, while she has won the League pennant six times, Boston three times and Providence twice.

The record of 1887 will be found at the end of the statistical tables of the Eastern and Western tours made in 1887:

THE WORLD'S CHAMPIONSHIP.

THE LEAGUE CHAMPIONS VS. THE AMERICAN CHAMPIONS.

The series of contests between the Detroit team, the champions of the League in 1887, and the St. Louis team, the champions of American Association the same year, unquestionably settled the fact that a supplementary series of championship matches had become a necessary adjunct of each season's contests in the League and American Association championship arena in order to end all doubt as to which club team of the two leading professional organizations was entitled to the honor of being the champion team of the United States. Up to 1884 this question of what is now justly termed the "world's championship" in baseball, remained an unsettled one; each organization being content to claim their leading teams as "champions of the United States" without having established the right to the title. But at the close of the season of 1884 the inaugural contest for the world's championship took place, though it was an informal exhibition series, the Metropolitan champions of the American Association of 1884 entering the lists in October of that year, against the Providence champions of the League in a series of best two out of three games, the Providence team winning without difficulty, as the appended record shows.

Oct. 23, Providence vs. Metropolitan, at the Polo Grounds............ 6—0
Oct. 24,   "   "   "   "   "   "   .... 3—1
Oct. 25,   "   "   "   "   "   "   ....12—2

Total.. 21—3

In 1885 the first regular series of these supplememtary championship contests took place, the contestants being the League champion team of Chicago, and the St. Louis champions of the American Association. In this series $1,000 was the prize competed for, and as neither team won the series each club received $500 of the prize money, each winning three games after the first game had been drawn the series being best four games in seven. The record of these games is appended:

Oct. 14, St. Louis vs. Chicago, at Chicago (8 innings)................ 5—5
Oct. 15, Chicago vs. St. Louis, at St. Louis (6 innings) forfeited...... 5—4
Oct. 16, St. Louis vs. Chicago, at St. Louis.......................... 7—4
Oct. 17, St. Louis vs. Chicago, at St. Louis.......................... 3—2
Oct. 22, Chicago vs. St. Louis, at Pittsburg (7 innings).............. 9—2
Oct. 23, Chicago vs. St. Louis, at Cincinnati......................... 9—2
Oct. 24, St. Louis vs. Chicago, at Cincinnati.........................13—4

Total victories for Chicago, 3; for St. Louis, 3, with one game drawn. Total runs scored by Chicago, 43; by St. Louis, 41.

In the contest of Oct. 15, at St. Louis, the umpire awarded the game to Chicago in the sixth innings by 9 to 0, and this award was concurred in by the St. Louis club. It may be well to add that there was not on either side the slightest dispute or difference of claim as to the equal division of the $1,000 on the basis of a tie.

BASE BALL GUIDE. 47

In 1886 the Chicago and St. Louis club teams again won the championship honors of their respective associations, and they again entered the lists for the "world's championship," this series being best out of six games, three being played at Chicago and three at St. Louis; the winner of the series taking all the gate receipts. The result was the success of the St. Louis team, the scores being as follows:

Oct. 18, Chicago vs. St. Louis, at Chicago........................... 6—0
Oct. 19, St. Louis vs. Chicago, at Chicago (8 innings)............... 12—0
Oct. 20, Chicago vs. St. Louis, at Chicago (8 innings).............. 11—4
Oct. 21, St. Louis vs. Chicago, at St. Louis (7 innings).......... 8—5
Oct. 22, St. Louis vs. Chicago, at St. Louis (6 innings)............ 10—3
Oct. 23, St. Louis vs. Chicago, at St. Louis (10 innings)............ 4—3

Total runs for St. Louis, 38; for Chicago, 29.

In 1887 the world's championship series had become an established supplementary series of contests, and in this year these contests excited more interest than had previously been manifested in regard to them, the demands made upon the two contesting teams —the Detroit champions of the League and the St. Louis champions of the American Association—for a game of the series from the large cities of the East and West being such as to lead the two clubs to extend the series to one of best out of fifteen games. These were played at St. Louis, Detroit, Chicago, and Pittsburg in the West, and at New York, Brooklyn, Boston, Philadelphia and Baltimore in the East. The series began in St. Louis, and the eighth victory of the Detroits was won at Baltimore, St. Louis winning the last game of the series at St. Louis. The record of the fifteen games, showing the pitchers in each contest, is as follows:

Date.	Contesting Clubs.	Cities.	Pitch'rs		Innings	Score.
Oct. 10	St. Louis v. Detroit....	St. Louis....	Carruthers...	Getzein	9	6-1
" 11	Detroit v. St. Louis....	St. Louis....	Conway......	Foutz	9	5-3
" 12	" v. "	....Detroit......	Getzein...	Carruthers	13	2-1
" 13	" v. "	....Pittsburg....	Baldwin.......	King	9	8-0
" 14	St. Louis v. Detroit....	Brooklyn ...	Carruthers..	Conway	9	5-2
" 15	Detroit v. St. Louis....	New York..	Getzein.......	Foutz	9	9-0
" 17	" v. "	....Philadelp'a.	Baldwin..	Carruth'rs	9	3-1
" 18	" v. "	....Boston......	Baldwin.	Carruth'rs	9	9-2
" 19	" v. "	....Philadelp'a.	Conway......	King	9	4-2
" 21	St. Louis v. Detroit....	Washington	Carruthers...	Getzein	9	11-4
" 22	Detroit v. St. Louis....	Baltimore....	Baldwin.....	Foutz	9	13-3
" 24	" v. "	.... Detroit......	Baldwin..	Carruth'rs	9	6-3
" 25	" v. "	.... Chicago.....	Getzein.......	King	9	4-3
" 26	St. Louis v. Detroit....	St. Louis ...	Carruthers..	Baldwin	6	9-2

The statistical record of the series of fifteen games is appended.

BATTING AND FIELDING AVERAGES.

DETROIT.

Rank.	Players.	Games.	T. B.	R.	B. H.	P. O.	Times Assisted.	E.	Batting Per Cent.	Fielding Per Cent.
1	Thompson, rf	15	61	8	21	22	2	1	.344	.960
2	Rowe, ss	15	65	12	19	24	53	9	.292	.895
3	Bennett, c	11	45	6	12	61	11	4	.267	.947
4	Getzein, p	6	23	5	6	2	30	3	.261	.914
5	Twitchell, lf	7	24	5	5	8	2	1	.208	.909
6	White, 3b	15	60	8	12	31	44	9	.200	.893
7	Ganzel, 1b, c	14	60	5	12	113	11	7	.200	.947
8	Richardson, lf, 2b	15	67	12	12	31	22	6	.180	.900
9	Hanlon, cf	15	56	5	10	35	1	1	.179	.973
10	Dunlap, 2b	10	38	5	6	33	27	2	.158	.967
11	Baldwin, p	5	19	1	3	1	12	4	.153	.765
12	Conway, p	4	12	0	0	1	14	0	.000	1.000
13	Sutcliffe, 1b	3	12	1	1	29	2	3	.083	.912
14	Brouthers, 1b	1	3	0	2	5	0	0	.667	1.000
		15	545	73	121	396	231	50	.240	.926

ST. LOUIS.

Rank.	Players.	Games.	T. B.	R.	B. H.	P. O.	Times Assisted.	E.	Batting Per cent.	Fielding Per cent.
1	Comiskey, 1 b	15	63	8	18	146	5	3	.286	.981
2	Latham, 3 b	15	67	12	17	20	28	9	.254	.842
3	Carruthers, p. rf	11	48	2	11	17	29	4	.229	.918
4	Robinson, 2 b	15	57	5	13	32	69	8	.228	.927
5	Boyle, c	6	24	1	3	39	8	8	.208	.885
6	Welch, cf	15	59	6	12	28	3	4	.204	.886
7	O'Nei', lf	15	65	7	13	25	3	3	.200	.903
8	Bushong, c	9	32	3	6	35	10	10	.188	.818
9	Foutz, rf, p	15	61	4	10	25	13	1	.164	.974
10	Gleason, ss	13	57	3	8	17	33	17	.140	.746
11	King, p	4	14	0	1	2	21	0	.071	.000
12	Lyons, ss	2	8	3	2	2	5	3	.250	1.700
	Totals	15	555	54	117	389	229	70	.211	.898

CLUB BATTING.

CLUBS.	Games.	A. B.	R.	B. H.	Average.
Detroit	15	544	72	147	.270
St. Louis	15	547	54	143	.262

CLUB FIELDING.

CLUBS.	Games.	P. O.	Assists.	E.	Total Chances.	Per cent. Accept'd.
Detroit	15	364	217	43	624	.931
St. Louis	15	389	236	68	693	.902

THE PITCHERS' WORK.

PLAYERS.	Games.	Base Hits off the Pitchers.				Base on Balls.	Runs earned.	Struck Out.	Hit by pitch'r.	Wild pitches.
		1 B.	2 B.	3 B.	H. R.					
Getzein	6	75	5	2	2	15	21	11	2	5
Conway	4	36	4	1	0	8	7	8	3	2
Baldwin	5	34	6	4	1	7	5	4	2	1
Carruthers	8	71	4	5	3	15	14	13	0	5
Foutz	3	43	5	1	1	9	8	5	1	2
King	4	27	3	4	0	1	8	21	0	2

DETROIT.

PLAYERS.	Games.	R.	B. H.	Runs Earned.	Base on Balls.	Wild Pitches.	Struck Out.	Average Runs to Game.	Average Hits to Game.
Baldwin	5	16	24	5	10	0	4	3.20	4.80
Conway	4	15	30	5	7	2	10	3.75	7.50
Getzein	6	23	63	15	15	3	17	3.83	10.50
Totals	15	54	117	25	32	5	31	3.60	7.80

ST. LOUIS.

PLAYERS.	Games.	R.	B. H.	Runs Earned.	Base on Balls.	Wild Pitches.	Struck Out.	Average Runs to Game.	Average Hits to Game.
King	4	17	26	7	1	2	21	4.25	6.50
Carruthers	8	29	63	12	12	4	17	3.62	7.87
Foutz	3	27	32	7	9	1	6	9.00	10.66
Totals	15	73	121	26	22	7	44	4.86	8.06

CATCHERS' WORK.

Passed Balls.—Bennett, 5 ; Ganzel, 10 ; Sutcliffe, 0 ; Bushong 9 ; Boyle, 6.

BASE RUNNING.

Stolen Bases.—Richardson, 7; Ganzel, 5; Rowe, 4; Thompson 4; White, 2 ; Dunlap, 3 ; Bennett, 4 ; Hanlon, 8 ; Baldwin, 1 Getzein, 1 ; Twitchell, 1; Total, 40.

Latham, 17; Comiskey, 4 ; Gleason, 1 ; Foutz, 1 ; Welch, 1; Robinson, 3; Carruthers, 3. Total, 30.

The clean base hits—not counting base hits on called balls— were 95 for St. Louis against 89 for Detroit.

THE LEAGUE PITCHING OF 1887.

The scoring rules of the national code of playing rules of the game in 1887 were of such a character as to entirely prevent the figures of the pitcher's records, as sent in by the official scorers, from being of any use in forming correct data for reliable averages at the close of the season. In fact, so full of blunders was the scoring data, as far as the pitching and batting was concerned, that every effort to judge of a pitcher's skill, on the basis of runs earned off his pitching, or of clean base hits made from it, proved as futile as did the effort to judge of his fielding skill by the figures of the fielding averages. How is it possible to make the pitching averages a criterion of a pitcher's skill in his position, when those averages are based on such data as base hits on called balls? Such hits, too, being so mixed up with the figures of clean hits as to make a distinction in the averages impossible? Inasmuch as earned runs, too, were scored on the basis of having base hits on called balls a factor in estimating them, the earned run averages became equally unreliable.

In regard to judging of a pitcher's ability as a fielder in his position by the fielding averages of pitchers, the basis was made equally as unreliable as the estimate of earned runs was, owing to the fact that the data of the fielding averages of a pitcher were made up from the figures of "assistances on strikes" as well as from legitimate fielding assistances. For this reason the pitcher, who was really a poor fielder in his position in fielding balls from the bat, but who happened to be fortunate in striking batsmen out by his pitching—thereby getting a big record of pitching assistances—became the leader in the pitcher's fielding averages; while the pitcher who really excelled as a fielder when in the box, but who was not as fortunate in striking out his batting opponents, and therefore could not furnish as good a record of assistances on strikes, was set down in the fielding averages as a tail-ender. Under these circumstances there remains but one estimate of a pitcher's skill left as a guide in judging of the pitching done in the League during 1887, and that is to make his percentage of victories he pitched in during the season, the sole criterion of his ability in the box. No other data are left to judge him by, for—as above shown—neither the averages of runs earned off his pitching, or of base hits made from it are worth the paper they are printed on, for any such purpose. In view of this fact we prepared for the GUIDE for 1887 a complete table showing the victories and defeats each pitcher pitched in against the opposing seven club teams each had to face during the championship season, the limit of names being set at those pitchers who failed to pitch in less than five victories. The pitching tables not only present a tolerably fair criterion of a pitcher's skill in the box—though of course not as reliable as the data of clean earned runs off his pitching or of clean hits made from it—but they afford an interesting and instructive record from which to judge of the success of a pitcher in defeating one particular team more frequently than he does another, and vice versa. For instance, it will be seen by a glance at the appended tables that pitcher Clarkson of the Chicago team, who pitched in nine victories against the Detroit team out of thirteen he pitched in against them, when facing the Pittsburgh team, was only successful in one out of eight games he pitched in against the latter team. Again in the instance of Keefe's pitching, while he could only pitch in one victory out of seven games he pitched in against the Chicago team, he pitched in no less than six victories out of the seven games he pitched in against the Pittsburg team. In fact, experience has shown that no matter how effective a pitcher may be in a season's work, it will be found that there is always one team which bothers him more than any other he has to face, just as shown in the above quoted instances. The appended tables show the record of victories and defeats in which every prominent League pitcher pitched in who was successful in not less than five games. They present by far the most interesting pitching statistics ever presented in the League GUIDE, and will serve as a valuable reference for the season of 1888.

VICTORIES, 1887—LEAGUE.

PITCHERS.	Detroit.	Philadelphia.	Chicago.	New York.	Boston.	Pittsburg.	Washington.	Indianapolis.	Victories.
Clarkson	9	8	....	7	4	1	4	5	38
Keefe	6	4	1	....	6	6	5	7	35
Casey	6	....	3	2	4	4	3	6	28
Getzein	....	3	4	5	3	5	4	4	28
Galvin	2	3	6	4	3	....	3	6	27

VICTORIES, 1887.—CONTINUED.

PITCHERS.	Detroit	Philadelphia	Chicago	New York	Boston	Pittsburg	Washington	Indianapolis	Victories
Whitney	3	1	3	4	5	5	....	4	25
Radbourne	4	3	4	3	....	4	3	6	24
Ferguson	1	....	1	4	4	5	4	5	24
Welch	0	2	5	....	4	5	1	6	23
Madden	3	4	1	3	....	3	3	4	21
Buffinton	1	....	2	3	1	3	5	6	21
Baldwin, (Chicago)	1	3	....	2	3	2	2	6	19
Morris	0	3	3	1	1	....	4	3	15
McCormick	2	0	3	1	3	....	2	2	13
Boyle	0	1	3	1	3	2	3	....	13
Baldwin, (Detroit)	....	1	1	2	2	2	2	3	13
Weidman	....	2	1	1	1	3	2	3	12
Healy	0	0	2	0	2	4	4	....	12
Twitchell	.	1	1	1	2	2	1	3	11
Van Haltren	0	0	....	2	2	2	3	1	10
Conway, (Buffalo)	0	1	2	1	....	2	2	2	10
Conway, (Detroit)	....	2	1	1	1	1	1	1	8
O'Day	0	0	3	1	1	0	....	4	8
Gilmore	1	0	0	1	2	3	....	0	7
Shaw	0	2	1	2	0	1	....	0	6
Stemmyer	0	1	0	0	....	1	2	2	6
Shreve	3	0	0	1	1	0	0	....	5

DEFEATS—1887.

PITCHERS.	Detroit	Philadelphia	Chicago	New York	Boston	Pittsburg	Washington	Indianapolis	Defeats
Twitchell	....	0	0	0	1	0	0	0	1
Van Haltren	1	0	....	2	1	1	1	1	7
Weidman	....	2	3	1	0	1	0	0	7
Stemmyer	2	2	1	1	....	2	0	0	8
Conway, (Detroit)	....	6	1	1	1	1	1	3	9
Shreve	2	2	2	1	2	0	0	....	9
Baldwin, (Detroit)	....	2	1	4	2	1	0	0	10
Ferguson	3	....	3	0	2	2	0	1	11
Getzein	....	3	4	1	2	1	2	0	13
Casey	2	....	4	3	1	2	1	0	13
Shaw	3	0	3	2	2	1	....	2	13
Madden	2	1	3	4	....	1	1	2	14
Welch	1	3	2	....	2	2	4	1	15
Buffinton	4	....	3	3	3	1	1	0	15
Conway, (Buffalo)	3	3	2	0	....	2	1	4	15
Baldwin, (Chicago)	2	6	....	2	1	2	3	1	17
Keefe	4	3	6	....	3	1	2	0	19
O'Day	4	2	3	3	2	3	....	2	19

DEFEATS, 1887.—CONTINUED.

PITCHERS.	Detroit.	Philadelphia.	Chicago.	New York.	Boston.	Pittsburg.	Washington.	Indianapolis.	Defeats.
Clarkson	4	0	....	2	4	7	2	1	20
Gilmore	3	5	2	2	2	4	....	2	20
Galvin	5	3	1	3	4	....	3	2	21
Whitney	2	6	3	2	3	1	....	4	21
Morris	5	3	3	2	4	....	3	2	22
Boyle	4	3	3	4	2	5	2	....	23
McCormick	1	6	1	7	3	....	3	2	23
Radbourne	4	3	3	5	....	4	3	1	23
Healy	3	4	4	6	4	4	3	....	28

The correct estimate of the pitcher's skill in pitching in victories is, of course, the record of his percentage of victories, which is appended:

PER CENT. OF VICTORIES PITCHED IN.

Rank.	PITCHERS.	CLUBS.	Games.	Victories.	Defeats.	Per cent. of Victories.
1	Twitchell	Detroit	12	11	1	.917
2	Ferguson	Philadelphia	35	24	11	.686
3	Casey	Philadelphia	41	28	13	.683
4	Getzein	Detroit	41	28	13	.683
5	Clarkson	Chicago	58	38	20	.655
6	Keefe	New York	54	35	19	.648
7	Weidman	Detroit	19	12	7	.632
8	Welch	New York	38	23	15	.605
9	Madden	Boston	35	21	14	.600
10	Van Haltren	Chicago	17	10	7	.588
11	Buffinton	Philadelphia	36	21	15	.583
12	Baldwin	Detroit	23	13	10	.565
13	Galvin	Pittsburg	48	27	21	.563
14	Whitney	Washington	46	25	21	.543
15	Baldwin	Chicago	36	19	17	.528
16	Radbourne	Boston	47	24	23	.510
17	Conway	Detroit	17	8	9	.471
18	Stemmyer	Boston	14	6	8	.429
19	Morris	Pittsburg	37	15	22	.405
20	Conway	Boston	25	10	15	.400
21	McCormick	Pittsburg	36	13	23	.361
22	Boyle	Indianapolis	36	13	23	.361
23	Shreve	Detroit	14	5	9	.357
24	Shaw	Washington	19	6	13	.316
25	Healy	Indianapolis	40	12	28	.300
26	O'Day	Washington	27	8	19	.296
27	Gilmore	Washington	27	7	20	.259

All the other League pitchers had a credit of less than five victories.

THE CLUB PITCHING RECORD.

The record of the pitching done by all the pitchers of each club in the League of 1887, will be found in the appended tables:

CLUB RECORD.

OF VICTORIES AND PITCHED IN.

WESTERN CLUB PITCHERS.

DETROIT.

PITCHERS.	Detroit.	Philadelphia.	Chicago.	New York.	Boston.	Pittsburg.	Washington.	Indianapolis.	Victories.
Getzein....................	....	3	4	5	3	5	4	4	28
Baldwin....................	....	1	1	2	2	2	2	3	13
Weidman...................	....	2	1	1	1	3	2	3	13
Twitchell...................	....	1	1	1	2	2	1	3	11
Conway....................	....	2	1	1	1	1	1	1	8
Gruber.....................	....	0	0	0	2	0	2	0	4
Beatin.....................	....	0	0	0	0	1	0	0	1
Burke......................	....	0	0	0	0	0	1	0	1
Totals..................		9	8	10	11	14	13	14	79

CHICAGO.

PITCHERS.	Detroit.	Philadelphia.	Chicago.	New York.	Boston.	Pittsburg.	Washington.	Indianapolis.	Victories.
Clarkson...................	9	8	....	7	4	1	4	5	38
Baldwin....................	1	3	....	2	3	2	2	6	19
Van Haltren................	0	0	....	2	2	2	3	1	10
Ryan.......................	0	1	....	0	0	0	1	0	2
Pyle.......................	0	0	....	0	0	0	0	1	1
Sprague....................	0	0	....	0	0	1	1	0	1
Totals..................	10	12	....	11	9	5	11	13	71

PITTSBURG.

PITCHERS.	Detroit.	Philadelphia.	Chicago.	New York.	Boston.	Pittsburg.	Washington.	Indianapolis.	Victories.
Galvin.................	2	3	6	4	3	....	3	6	27
Morris.................	0	3	3	1	1	....	4	3	15
McCormick.............	2	0	3	1	3	....	2	2	13
Totals...............	4	6	12	6	7		9	11	55

INDIANAPOLIS.

PITCHERS.	Detroit.	Philadelphia.	Chicago.	New York.	Boston.	Pittsburg.	Washington.	Indianapolis.	Victories.
Boyle...............	0	1	3	1	3	2	3	....	13
Healy...............	0	0	2	0	2	4	4	....	12
Shreve..............	3	0	0	1	1	0	0	....	5
Morrison............	0	0	0	0	1	0	2	....	3
Leitner.............	1	0	0	1	0	0	0	....	2
Moffat..............	0	0	0	0	0	0	1	....	1
Kirby...............	0	0	0	0	0	1	0	....	1
Totals..............	4	1	5	3	7	7	10		37

EASTERN CLUB PITCHERS.

PHILADELPHIA.

PITCHERS.	Detroit.	Philadelphia.	Chicago.	New York.	Boston.	Pittsburg.	Washington.	Indianapolis.	Victories.
Casey...............	6	....	3	2	4	4	3	6	28
Ferguson............	1	....	1	4	4	5	4	5	24
Buffinton...........	1	....	2	3	1	3	5	6	21
Maul................	0	....	0	1	0	0	1	0	2
Totals..............	8		6	10	9	12	13	17	75

NEW YORK.

PITCHERS.	Detroit.	Philadelphia.	Chicago.	New York.	Boston.	Pittsburg.	Washington.	Indianapolis.	Victories.
Keefe.............................	6	4	1	....	6	6	5	7	35
Welch.............................	0	2	5	....	4	5	1	6	23
Titcomb...........................	2	0	0	....	0	0	2	0	4
Mattimore.........................	0	1	0	....	0	0	1	1	3
George............................	0	0	0	....	0	1	1	1	3
Totals............................	8	7	6		10	12	10	15	68

BOSTON.

PITCHERS.	Detroit.	Philadelphia.	Chicago.	New York.	Boston.	Pittsburg.	Washington.	Indianapolis.	Victories.
Radbourne........................	4	3	4	3	....	4	3	6	24
Madden............................	3	4	1	3	....	3	3	4	21
Conway............................	0	1	2	1	....	2	2	2	10
Stemmyer..........................	0	1	0	0	....	1	2	2	6
Totals............................	7	9	7	7		10	10	14	61

WASHINGTON.

PITCHERS.	Detroit.	Philadelphia.	Chicago.	New York.	Boston.	Pittsburg.	Washington.	Indianapolis.	Victories.
Whitney...........................	3	1	3	4	5	5	....	4	25
O'Day.............................	0	0	3	1	0	0	....	4	8
Gilmore...........................	1	0	0	1	2	3	....	0	7
Shaw..............................	0	2	1	2	0	1	....	0	6
Totals............................	4	3	7	8	7	9		8	46

LEAGUE VS. AMERICAN.

The victories scored in the exhibition campaign of 1887 by the League Clubs were as follows:

BASE BALL GUIDE.

	Cincinnati.	Brooklyn.	Louisville.	Metropolitan.	Baltimore.	Cleveland.	Athletic.	St. Louis.	Won.	Played.
Detroit	0	0	1	0	0	0	0	10	11	16
Philadelphia	0	0	0	0	0	0	9	0	9	16
Indianapolis	0	0	2	0	0	3	0	2	7	17
Washington	0	0	0	2	3	0	0	0	5	8
Chicago	1	0	0	0	0	0	0	4	5	10
Boston	0	2	0	0	2	0	0	0	4	5
Pittsburg	0	0	0	0	0	3	0	0	3	3
New York	0	0	0	1	0	0	0	0	1	2
Lost	1	2	3	3	5	6	9	16	45	77

Those scored by the American Association clubs are appended:

	Pittsburg.	Boston.	New York.	Washington.	Detroit.	Chicago.	Philadelphia.	Indianapolis.	Won.	Played.
Cincinnati	0	0	0	0	0	3	0	6	9	10
St. Louis	0	0	0	0	5	2	0	1	8	24
Athletic	0	0	0	0	0	0	7	0	7	16
Baltimore	0	1	1	1	0	0	0	0	3	8
Cleveland	0	0	0	1	0	0	0	2	3	9
Louisville	0	0	0	0	0	0	0	1	1	4
Metropolitan	0	0	0	1	0	0	0	0	1	4
Brooklyn	0	0	0	0	0	0	0	0	0	2
Lost	0	1	1	3	5	5	7	10	32	77

THE LEAGUE AVERAGES FOR 1887.

The following are the official averages of the players of the eight League Clubs of 1887, giving the names of Players who took part in fifteen championship contests or more during the season.

BATTING AVERAGES.

Rank.	NAME.	CLUB.	Games Played.	Times at Bat.	Runs Scored.	Ave. per Game.	First Base Hits.	Percentage.	Total Bases.	Ave. per Game.	Bases Stolen.	Ave. per Game.
1	Maul........	Philadelphia..	16	71	15	0.93	32	.450	41	2.56	5	0.31
2	Anson.......	Chicago......	122	532	107	0.87	224	.421	308	2.52	27	0.22
3	Brouthers....	Detroit......	122	570	153	1.25	239	.419	340	2.78	34	0.27
4	Ferguson....	Philadelphia..	69	298	66	0.95	123	.412	161	2.33	13	0.18
5	Darling......	Chicago......	38	163	27	0.71	67	.411	84	2.21	19	0.50
6	Thompson...	Detroit......	127	576	118	0.92	234	.406	344	2.70	2	0.17
7	Kelly.......	Boston.......	114	525	119	1.04	207	.394	286	2.50	84	0.73
8	Shomberg...	Indianapolis..	112	475	91	0.81	185	.389	247	2.11	21	0.18
9	Connor......	New York....	127	546	113	0.89	209	.382	329	2.59	43	0.34
10	Wise........	Boston.......	110	491	95	0.86	187	.380	275	2.50	43	0.39
10	Carroll......	Pittsburg.....	101	457	71	0.70	174	.380	235	2.32	23	0.22
11	Ward........	New York....	129	574	113	0.87	213	.371	245	1.89	111	0.86
11	Williamson..	Chicago......	127	512	77	0.60	190	.371	262	2.06	45	0.35
12	Hines........	Washington..	123	526	83	0.67	195	.370	264	2.14	46	0.37
13	Nash........	Boston.......	118	521	98	0.83	192	.368	247	2.09	49	0.41
14	Fogarty.....	Philadelphia..	126	577	112	0.81	211	.365	280	2.22	102	0.80
14	McKinnon...	Pittsburg.....	48	208	25	0.52	76	.365	106	2.21	6	0.12
14	Ewing.......	New York....	76	348	81	1.06	127	.365	180	2.37	36	0.47
15	Richardson..	Detroit......	120	573	130	1.08	208	.363	288	2.40	29	0.24
15	Bennett.....	"	46	190	26	0.56	69	.363	94	2.04	7	0.15
15	Rowe........	"	123	575	134	1.08	209	.363	267	2.17	22	0.18
16	Deasley.....	New York....	29	127	13	0.45	46	.362	51	1.76	2	0.07
17	Sunday......	Chicago......	48	220	41	0.85	79	.359	100	2.08	34	0.70
18	Ryan........	"	126	556	117	0.92	198	.355	259	2.05	50	0.39
19	McGuire.....	Philadelphia..	40	161	22	0.55	57	.354	77	1.92	3	0.07
19	Andrews....	"	103	485	108	1.05	172	.354	218	2.11	57	0.54
20	Twitchell....	Detroit......	63	272	43	0.68	96	.352	120	1.90	12	0.19
21	Glasscock...	Indianapolis..	121	524	91	0.75	183	.349	217	1.79	62	0.51
21	Rainy.......	New York....	17	63	5	0.29	22	.349	24	1.41	0	0.00
22	Gore........	"	111	500	95	0.85	174	.348	201	1.81	39	0.35
23	Baldwin.....	Detroit......	24	95	15	0.62	33	.347	35	1.45	4	0.16
24	Farrar......	Philadelphia..	115	485	83	0.72	167	.344	214	1.86	24	0.21
24	O'Rourke...	New York....	103	433	73	0.70	149	.344	190	1.84	46	0.44
25	Whitney.....	Pittsburg.....	119	486	56	0.47	167	.343	191	1.60	10	0.08
26	Wood........	Philadelphia..	113	531	118	1.04	182	.342	275	2.43	19	0.17
27	White.......	Detroit......	111	474	71	0.64	162	.341	206	1.85	20	0.17
28	Tiernan.....	New York....	103	438	81	0.78	149	.340	210	2.04	28	0.27
28	Denny.......	Indianapolis..	122	523	86	0.70	178	.340	266	2.18	29	0.24
28	Shindle.....	Detroit......	20	91	17	0.85	31	.340	38	1.90	13	0.65
29	Irwin........	Philadelphia..	99	422	64	0.64	143	.339	179	1.80	19	0.19
30	Sullivan....	Chicago......	115	538	98	0.85	170	.334	229	1.99	35	0.30
30	Coleman.....	Pittsburg.....	115	505	75	0.65	169	.334	216	1.87	25	0.21

BASE BALL GUIDE.   59

BATTING RECORD.—*Continued*.

Rank.	NAME.	CLUB.	Games Played.	Times at Bat.	Runs Scored.	Ave. per Game.	First Base Hits.	Percentage.	Total Bases.	Ave. per Game.	Bases Stolen.	Ave. per Game.
31	Richardson..	New York.....	122	485	79	0.64	161	.333	210	1.72	41	0.33
32	Morrill......	Boston........	124	528	79	0.63	175	.331	251	2.02	19	0.15
33	Sutton......	"	74	327	57	0.77	108	.327	144	1.94	17	0.23
34	Seery.......	Indianapolis..	122	536	104	0.85	175	.326	229	1.79	.48	0.39
	Dunlap......	Detroit........	64	297	60	0.93	97	.326	144	2.25	15	0.23
35	Pfeffer......	Chicago....	123	513	95	0.77	167	.325	244	1.98	57	0.46
36	Whitney.....	Washington..	52	219	29	0.55	71	.324	98	1.88	10	0.19
37	Kuhne.......	Pittsburg......	101	416	68	0.67	134	.322	179	1.77	17	0.16
38	Conway......	Boston........	39	150	21	0.54	48	.320	54	1.38	5	0.12
39	Burns	Chicago.....	115	460	57	0.49	146	.317	190	1.65	32	0.27
	Mulvey......	Philadelphia..	109	495	94	0.86	157	.317	191	1.75	43	0.39
40	Hanlon......	Detroit........	118	500	79	0.66	158	.316	194	1.64	69	0.58
41	Wheelock...	Boston........	44	181	30	0.68	57	.314	65	1.47	20	0.45
42	Miller.......	Pittsburg.....	87	377	57	0.65	118	.313	146	1.67	33	0.38
43	O'Brien......	Washington..	113	474	70	0.62	147	.310	235	2.08	11	0.09
44	Myers........	"	105	402	45	0.43	124	.308	150	1.43	18	0.17
45	Clements....	Philadelphia..	63	255	48	0.76	78	.306	103	1.63	7	0.11
	Gardner.....	Indianapolis..	18	75	8	0.44	23	.306	26	1.44	7	0.39
46	Burdock.....	Boston........	64	259	33	0.51	79	.305	83	1.29	19	0.29
	Madden.....	"	37	141	23	0.62	44	.305	53	1.43	6	0.16
47	Kreig........	Washington..	24	102	9	0.37	31	.304	45	1.87	2	0.08
48	Pettit........	Chicago......	32	146	29	0.90	44	.301	59	1.84	16	0.50
49	Dalrymple...	Pittsburg.....	92	403	43	0.46	121	.300	154	1.67	29	0.31
50	Hornung.....	Boston........	97	451	84	0.86	135	.299	172	1.77	41	0.42
51	Fields.......	Pittsburg.....	39	171	27	0.69	51	.298	64	1.64	7	0.18
	Daily........	Phila. & Wash	105	443	58	0.55	132	.298	181	1.72	26	0.25
52	Radbourne ..	Boston........	48	185	24	0.50	55	.297	64	1.33	6	0.12
53	Buffinton....	Philadelphia..	66	280	34	0.51	83	.296	100	1.51	8	0.12
54	Dorgan.......	New York....	71	298	41	0.57	88	.295	101	1.42	22	0.31
55	Schock......	Washington..	69	285	47	0.68	84	.294	98	1.42	29	0.42
56	Gunning....	Philadelphia..	27	109	22	0.81	32	.293	42	1.55	18	0.66
	Keefe........	New York....	56	211	26	0.52	62	.293	86	1.72	2	0.04
	Gillespie	"	74	307	40	0.54	90	.293	114	1.54	37	0.50
57	Barkley......	Pittsburg...	90	370	43	0.47	106	.286	123	1.36	6	0.06
	Dealy........	Washington..	56	220	33	0.59	63	.286	76	1.35	36	0.64
58	Ganzell......	Detroit........	55	285	40	0.72	67	.285	80	1.45	3	0.05
59	Myers.......	Indianapolis..	66	257	25	0.38	73	.284	86	1.30	26	0.39
60	Johnston.....	Boston........	124	511	88	0.71	145	.283	212	1.71	52	0.42
61	Flint.........	Chicago......	48	191	22	0.45	54	.282	82	1.70	7	0.14
62	Clarkson	"	61	226	40	0.65	63	.279	98	1.60	6	0.09
63	Van Haltren..	"	44	183	29	0.65	51	.278	64	1.45	12	0.27
	McGeachy...	Indianapolis..	99	410	49	0.49	114	.278	139	1.40	27	0.27
64	Briody.......	Detroit	32	137	22	0.68	38	.277	45	1.40	6	0.18
65	Carroll.......	Washington..	101	437	79	0.78	121	.276	160	1.58	40	0.39
66	Bastian......	Philadelphia..	60	240	34	0.56	66	.275	81	1.35	11	0.18
67	Beecher.....	Pittsburg. ..	40	176	15	0.37	48	.272	64	1.60	8	0.20
	Welch.......	New York....	40	154	16	0.40	42	.272	55	1.37	2	0.05
	Hackett.....	Indianapolis..	41	154	12	0.29	42	.272	57	1.39	4	0.09
8	Tate.........	Boston........	55	228	30	0.54	62	.271	70	1.27	7	0.12
69	Bassett......	Indianapolis..	119	477	41	0.34	129	.270	159	1.33	25	0.21

SPALDING'S OFFICIAL

BATTING RECORD.—Continued.

Rank	NAME.	CLUB.	Games Played.	Times at Bat.	Runs Scored.	Ave. per Game.	First Base Hits.	Percentage.	Total Bases.	Ave. per Game.	Bases Stolen.	Ave. per Game.
70	{ Shaw.......	Washington..	21	78	7	0.32	21	.269	23	1.04	1	0.04
	{ Daily........	Chicago......	74	278	45	0.60	75	.269	98	1.32	29	0.39
71	Farrell......	Washington..	86	359	40	0.46	95	.264	128	1.49	31	0.36
72	Smith.......	Pittsbug.....	122	486	70	0.57	128	.263	160	1.31	30	0.24
73	Brown ...	New York....	47	180	17	0.36	47	.261	54	1.14	10	0.21
74	{ Polhemus...	Indianapolis..	19	77	6	0.31	20	.259	21	1.10	4	0.21
	{ McLaughlin.	Philadelphia..	50	216	25	0.50	56	.259	76	1.52	2	0.04
75	Brown	Ind. & Pitts..	82	352	51	0.62	91	.258	112	1.36	21	0.25
76	McCormick..	Pittsburg.....	36	138	9	0.25	35	.253	42	1 16	0	0.00
77	Conway.....	Detroit..	24	97	16	0.66	24	.247	34	1 41	0	0.00
78	Murphy.....	New York....	16	57	4	0.25	14	.245	15	0.93	1	0.06
79	O'Day.......	Washington..	34	123	10	0.29	30	.244	33	0.97	2	0.06
80	Gilligan.....	"	27	95	7	0.26	23	.242	28	1.03	2	0.07
81	Baldwin.....	Chicago......	40	149	18	0.45	36	.241	51	1.27	4	0.10
82	{ Boyle.......	Indianapolis..	41	150	17	0 41	36	.240	50	1.22	2	0.05
	{ Getzein.....	Detroit......	43	166	19	0 44	40	.240	55	1.28	2	0.04
83	Arundel.....	Indianapolis..	43	165	13	0.30	39	.236	43	1.00	8	0.18
84	Cahill.......	"	68	272	22	0 31	63	.231	73	1.07	34	0.50
85	{ Morris......	Pittsburg.....	37	131	15	0 40	30	.229	35	0.94	1	0.02
	{ Donnelly ...	Washington..	117	441	51	0.43	101	.229	129	1.10	42	0.35
86	O'Rourke....	Boston........	21	85	12	0 57	19	.223	22	1.04	4	0.19
87	{ Galvin......	Pittsburg.....	49	195	13	0.26	43	.220	57	1.11	5	0.10
	{ Mack	Washington..	80	322	35	0.43	71	.220	81	1.01	26	0.32
	{ Weidman ...	Det. & N. Y..	21	86	11	0.52	19	.220	20	0.95	6	0.27
88	Daily........	Boston........	33	129	11	0.33	28	.217	33	1.00	7	0.21
89	{ McCarthy...	Philadelphia..	18	72	7	0.38	15	.208	18	1.00	15	0.83
	{ Tebeau.....	Chicago......	20	72	8	0.40	15	.208	17	0.85	8	0 40
90	Healy.......	Indianapolis..	40	142	14	0.35	28	.197	41	1 02	7	0.17
91	Casey.......	Philadelphia..	44	170	21	0.47	33	194	39	0.88	1	0.02
92	Gilmore.....	Washington..	27	100	4	0.15	13	130	13	0.48	2	0.07

THE VETERANS OF THE LEAGUE.

BATTING AVERAGES OF PLAYERS WHO HAVE TAKEN PART IN LEAGUE CHAMPIONSHIP GAMES FOR SIX OR MORE SEASONS 1876 TO 1887, BOTH INCLUSIVE.

Rank.	NAME.	Number of Seasons Played.	Number of Games Played.	Times at Bat.	First Base Hits.	Percentage.
1	Dennis Brouthers	8	716	3056	1107	.362
2	Adrian C. Anson	12	1039	4389	1574	.358
3	Rodger Connor	8	809	3389	1169	.345
4	M. J. Kelly	10	925	3931	1281	.326
5	Geo. F. Gore	9	822	3435	1101	.325
6	James O'Rourke	12	1026	4421	1347	.318
7	Paul A. Hines	12	1052	4599	1447	.314
7	James L. White	12	976	4083	1282	.314
8	Hardy Richardson	9	853	3708	1153	.311
9	J. C. Rowe	8	722	3097	942	.304
10	A. Dalrymple	10	853	3818	1148	.300
11	Wm. Ewing	7	537	2293	685	.298
12	Joseph Start	11	776	3366	995	.295
12	Fred Dunlap	7	626	2655	785	.295
13	E. B. Sutton	12	979	4086	1192	.291
14	John W. Glasscock	9	840	3405	970	.284
14	Geo. A. Wood	8	749	3248	925	.284
14	Sam W. Wise	6	594	2409	685	.284
15	George Shaffer	7	521	2137	602	.281
15	Thomas Burns	8	766	3114	875	.281
15	Chas. W. Bennett	9	637	2462	693	.281
16	P. Gillespie	8	703	2907	810	.278
17	M. C. Dorgan	9	660	2719	756	.277
18	E. N. Williamson	10	939	3711	1020	.275
18	Jno. A. Peters	6	384	1700	468	.275
18	Jno. E. Clapp	7	398	1688	465	.275
19	John F. Morrill	12	1060	4209	1157	.274
20	Jas. E. Whitney	7	483	1944	531	.273
21	Joseph Hornung	9	751	3275	885	.270
22	Thomas York	8	566	2291	617	.269
22	Robert Ferguson	8	538	2209	596	.269
23	Edwin Hanlon	8	785	3170	850	.268
24	Jeremiah Denny	7	698	2784	744	.267
24	Jno. M. Ward	8	924	3893	1041	.267

AVERAGES—*Continued.*

Rank.	NAME.	Number of Seasons Played.	Number of Games Played.	Times at Bat.	First Base Hits	Percentage.
26	Wm. M. Crowley	6	456	1796	474	.264
27	W. B. Phillips	6	529	2203	581	.263
28	P. J. Hotaling	6	514	2185	572	.261
28	W. A. Purcell	7	500	2136	559	.261
29	A. A. Irwin	8	672	2692	698	.259
30	J. E. Manning	6	485	2014	519	.257
31	John J. Burdock	12	850	3505	895	.255
32	Jno. Farrell	9	729	3048	776	.254
33	J. P. Cassidy	7	416	1718	433	.252
34	Chas. Radbourn	7	506	2013	500	.248
35	F. S. Flint	9	686	2682	655	.244
36	M. Welch	8	444	1648	401	.243
37	Jacob Evans	6	447	1737	413	.237
37	Jas. McCormick	10	499	1957	464	.237
38	Geo. W. Bradley	6	336	1319	311	.235
39	Jos. L. Quest	6	372	1459	333	.228
39	Chas. F. Briody	6	282	1043	238	.228
40	J. J. Gerhardt	7	565	2182	489	.224
41	Frank Hankinson	6	442	1671	369	.220
42	L. Corcoran	6	308	1227	265	.216
43	Jas. F. Galvin	8	474	1825	392	.215
44	B. Gilligan	9	510	1848	387	.209
45	D. W. Force	10	746	2873	598	.208
46	W. H. Holbert	6	286	1066	221	.207
47	Geo. E. Weidman	7	338	1273	222	.174

THE OFFICIAL AVERAGES OF 1887.

The following are the official statistics of the League season of 1887, prepared by President Young.

FIELDING AVERAGES.

Of Players who have taken part in fifteen or more championship games, SEASON OF 1887.

FIRST BASEMEN.

Rank	NAME	CLUB	Games Played	Number Put Out	Times Assisting	Fielding Errors	Total Chances	Percentage Accepted
1	Morrill	Boston	124	1202	47	18	1267	.985
2	Barkley	Pittsburg	53	557	15	12	584	.979
3	Conner	New York	127	1325	44	30	1399	.978
4	McKinnon	Pittsburg	48	488	25	12	525	.977
4	Farrar	Philadelphia	115	1149	46	28	1223	.977
5	Anson	Chicago	122	1232	70	36	1338	.973
6	O'Brien	Washington	103	1108	26	32	1166	.972
7	Brouthers	Detroit	122	1189	35	38	1262	.969
8	Shomberg	Indianapolis	112	1216	28	55	1299	.957
9	Carroll	Pittsburg	17	173	9	13	195	.933
0	Kreig	Washington	16	137	5	5	147	.932

SECOND BASEMEN.

Rank	NAME	CLUB	Games Played	Number Put Out	Times Assisting	Fielding Errors	Total Chances	Percentage Accepted
1	Dunlap	Detroit	64	208	217	21	446	.953
2	Ferguson	Philadelphia	25	59	67	7	133	.947
3	Richardson	Detroit	62	219	215	27	461	.941
4	Bassett	Indianapolis	119	273	414	53	740	.928
5	Richardson	New York	108	257	384	50	691	.927
6	Bastian	Philadelphia	39	79	128	18	225	.920
7	Pfeffer	Chicago	123	393	402	72	867	.916
8	Smith	Pittsburg	88	225	298	49	572	.914
9	Farrell	Washington	38	70	131	20	221	.909
10	Myers	"	78	193	246	44	483	.908
11	Barkley	Pittsburg	37	112	114	25	251	.900
12	Burdock	Boston	64	177	188	41	406	.899
13	McLaughlin	Philadelphia	50	110	156	33	299	.889
14	Kelly	Boston	32	83	105	35	223	.848
14	Ewing	New York	18	39	58	18	115	.848

THIRD BASEMEN.

Rank	NAME	CLUB	Games Played	Number Put Out	Times Assisting	Fielding Errors	Total Chances	Percentage Accepted
1	Whitney	Pittsburg	119	166	237	33	436	.924
2	Denny	Indianapolis	116	201	262	58	521	.888
3	Nash	Boston	114	204	236	58	498	.883
4	Burns	Chicago	107	168	246	61	475	.871
5	Tebeau	"	20	24	42	10	76	.868
6	Donnelly	Washington	115	136	275	63	474	.867
7	Mulvey	Philadelphia	109	123	197	50	370	.864
8	Ewing	New York	51	76	101	28	205	.863
9	White	Detroit	106	133	225	64	422	.848
10	Rainey	New York	17	17	26	8	51	.843
11	O'Rourke	"	36	46	50	18	114	.842
12	Shindle	Detroit	19	24	28	11	63	.825

SHORT STOPS.

Rank	NAME.	CLUB.	Games Played.	Number Put Out.	Times Assisting.	Fielding Errors.	Total Chances.	Percentage Accepted
1	Smith	Pittsburg	34	71	119	16	206	.922
2	Ward	New York	129	226	469	61	756	.919
3	Bastian	Philadelphia	17	20	44	6	70	.914
4	Glasscock	Indianapolis	121	211	493	73	777	.906
4	Rowe	Detroit	123	119	377	51	547	.906
5	Irwin	Philadelphia	99	178	301	58	537	.892
6	Williamson	Chicago	127	133	361	61	555	.890
7	Kuhne	Pittsburg	91	136	310	59	505	.883
8	Sutton	Boston	34	109	172	39	320	.878
8	Wheelock	"	17	33	68	14	115	.878
9	Farrell	Washington	48	91	156	35	282	.875
10	Wise	Boston	70	152	233	58	443	.869
11	Dealy	Washington	20	33	51	17	101	.831
12	Myers	"	27	51	93	33	177	.813

OUTFIELDERS.

Rank	NAME.	CLUB.	Games Played.	Number Put Out.	Times Assisting.	Fielding Errors.	Total Chances.	Percentage Accepted
1	Gillespie	New York	74	91	14	6	111	.946
2	Richardson	Detroit	58	109	8	8	125	.936
3	Ftelds	Pittsburg	28	54	4	4	62	.935
4	Hornung	Boston	97	192	23	15	230	.934
5	O'Rourke	New York	29	60	7	5	72	.930
5	Johnston	Boston	124	332	31	27	390	.930
6	Fogarty	Philadelphia	120	273	39	27	339	.920
7	Beecher	Pittsburg	40	84	12	9	105	.914
8	Thompson	Detroit	127	217	24	24	265	.909
9	VanHaltren	Chicago	26	35	3	4	42	.904
10	Hanlon	Detroit	118	264	18	30	312	.903
11	Andrews	Philadelphia	99	203	18	24	245	.902
12	Carroll	Washington	101	145	19	18	182	.901
13	Dalrymple	Pittsburg	92	184	14	22	220	.900
14	Coleman	"	114	214	17	26	257	.898
15	Schock	Washington	62	115	15	15	145	.896
16	M Geachy	Indianapolis	57	231	22	30	283	.894
17	Seery	"	122	220	25	30	275	.890
18	Gore	New York	111	221	20	30	271	.889
19	Hines	Washington	109	180	14	25	219	.885
20	Pettit	Chicago	32	36	9	6	51	.882
21	Sutton	Boston	18	21	0	3	24	.875
22	Wood	Philadelphia	105	155	10	24	189	.873
23	Dorgan	New York	69	128	6	20	154	.870
24	Twitchell	Detroit	52	82	3	13	98	.867
25	Tiernan	New York	101	150	10	25	185	.864
26	Brown	Pitts and Ind	82	188	18	33	239	.861
27	Wheelock	Boston	23	35	1	6	42	.857
28	Ryan	Chicago	120	164	33	33	230	.856
29	Darling	"	20	16	7	4	27	.851
30	Kelly	Boston	55	74	11	15	100	.850
31	Sullivan	Chicago	115	189	10	36	235	.846

Fielders' Averages—Continued.

Rank.	NAME.	CLUB.	Games Played.	Number Put Out.	Times Assisting.	Fielding Errors.	Total Chances.	Percentage Accepted.
32	Miller..........	Pittsburg...........	15	32	4	7	43	.837
33	Daily...........	Phila. and Wash....	98	140	13	30	183	.836
34	Carroll.........	Pittsburg...........	44	96	9	21	126	.833
35	Cahill..........	Indianapolis........	52	84	11	20	115	.826
36	Wise...........	Boston.............	26	39	7	10	56	.821
37	Sunday.........	Chicago............	48	78	4	25	107	.766
38	Buffinton.......	Philadelphia........	19	25	3	9	37	.756
39	Polhemus.......	Indianapolis........	19	21	8	10	39	.746

CATCHERS' AVERAGES.

Rank.	NAME.	CLUB.	Games Played.	Number Put Out.	Times Assisting.	Fielding Errors.	Passed Balls.	Total Chances.	Percentage Accepted.
1	Bennett.........	Detroit.............	46	198	51	10	16	275	.905
2	Tate............	Boston.............	50	198	102	25	24	349	.859
3	Clements........	Philadelphia.......	58	319	79	27	40	465	.856
4	Ganzell.........	Detroit.............	50	273	69	38	21	401	.852
4	Daily...........	Chicago............	65	354	148	40	47	589	.852
5	Briody..........	Detroit.............	32	136	51	21	12	220	.850
6	Flint............	Chicago............	46	255	73	26	37	391	.838
7	Murphy.........	New York..........	16	83	28	12	11	134	.828
8	Gunning.........	Philadelphia.......	27	133	55	21	20	229	.821
9	Miller...........	Pittsburg...........	71	265	62	28	46	401	.815
10	Brown...........	New York..........	45	231	74	23	51	379	.804
11	Myers...........	Indianapolis........	47	176	58	17	44	295	.793
12	Darling.........	Chicago............	18	117	37	17	24	195	.789
13	Dealy...........	Washington........	27	110	45	14	28	197	.786
14	Mack...........	"	73	389	126	55	88	658	.782
15	McGuire.........	Philadelphia.......	40	212	57	34	42	345	.779
15	Hackett.........	Indianapolis........	39	128	52	20	31	231	.779
16	O'Rourke.......	Boston.............	19	80	28	15	16	139	.777
17	Daily............	"	33	125	44	21	29	219	.771
17	Kelly............	"	22	80	35	15	19	149	.771
18	Carroll..........	Pittsburg...........	39	172	33	27	37	269	.762
19	Deasley.........	New York..........	24	92	32	20	19	163	.760
20	O'Rourke.......	"	37	137	66	18	47	268	.757
21	Gilligan.........	Washington........	24	88	40	16	28	172	.744
22	Arundel.........	Indianapolis........	42	153	64	32	48	297	.730

PITCHERS' RECORD IN ALPHABETICAL ORDER.

NAME.	CLUB.	Games Played.	Times at Bat of Opponents.	Runs Scored by Opponents.	Ave. per Game.	Runs earned by Opponents.	Ave. per Game.	First Base Hits Made by Opponents.	Percentage.	Number Put Out.	Times Assisting.	Fielding Errors.	Wild Pitches.	Total Chances.	Percentage Accepted.
Baldwin	Detroit	24	899	138	5.75	76	3.16	286	.318	7	91	8	7	113	.867
Boyle	Indianapolis	38	1394	200	5.26	92	2.42	479	.300	13	110	10	12	145	.848
Buffinton	Philadelphia	39	1472	233	5.97	129	3.31	471	.319	25	243	6	28	302	.887
Baldwin	Chicago	38	1464	224	5.89	115	3.02	472	.322	21	209	12	41	283	.812
Clarkson	"	58	2154	296	5.10	163	2.81	620	.287	33	360	13	25	430	.911
Conway	Detroit	17	621	87	5.12	40	2.35	173	.278	9	83	3	10	105	.876
Conway	Boston	25	971	157	6.28	85	3.40	336	.346	6	84	5	14	109	.825
Casey	Philadelphia	44	1657	213	4.84	118	2.68	498	.300	11	184	12	11	218	.894
Ferguson	"	33	1214	166	5.03	94	2.85	348	.286	15	181	10	10	216	.907
Gilmore	Washington	27	1035	169	6.26	97	3.59	347	.335	3	138	5	14	157	.898
Galvin	Pittsburg	49	1926	262	5.34	156	3.18	571	.296	22	189	13	20	238	.887
Getzein	Detroit	43	1597	228	5.30	145	3.37	490	.340	23	191	2	39	236	.906
Healy	Indianapolis	40	1453	269	6.72	146	3.65	495	.307	8	122	14	42	183	.710
Keefe	New York	56	1964	265	4.73	155	2.76	553	.281	21	274	15	16	352	.838
Madden	Boston	37	1397	210	5.67	100	2.70	437	.312	5	139	12	12	172	.837
Morris	Pittsburg	37	1383	225	6.08	140	3.78	443	.320	5	141	5	18	163	.845
McCormick	"	36	1405	217	6.03	131	3.64	446	.317	14	161	10	31	203	.862
O'Day	Washington	30	1111	194	6.47	94	3.13	362	.324	10	129	13	28	183	.759
Radbourne	Boston	48	1855	307	6.39	175	3.64	624	.336	13	156	14	4	208	.798
Shaw	Washington	21	842	180	8.57	118	5.62	307	.364	5	65	6	6	80	.575
VanHaltren	Chicago	18	569	102	5.66	55	3.05	226	.337	12	96	3	15	117	.914
Whitney	Washington	45	1713	258	5.61	123	2.67	490	.286	8	234	12	22	269	.899
Welch	New York	40	1448	192	4.80	116	2.90	428	.295	17	158	12	10	209	.837
Weidman	Det. and N.Y.	21	830	136	6.47	104	4.95	286	.344	5	88	11	10	114	.815

BATTING AND FIELDING.

Record of Clubs, Members of the National League of Professional B. B. Clubs.

SEASON OF 1887.

Rank.	NAME OF CLUB.	Games Played.	Games Won.	BATTING.									FIELDING.					
				Times at Bat.	Runs Scored.	Ave. per Game.	Runs Earned.	Ave. per Game.	First Base Hits.	Percentage.	Total Bases.	Ave. per Game.	Bases Stolen.	Ave. per Game.	Number Put Out.	Times Assisting.	Fielding Errors.	Passed Balls and Wild Pitches.	Total Chances.	Percentage Accepted.
1	Detroit......	126	79	5030	962	7.63	587	4.66	1749	.347	2354	18.68	266	2.11	3304	1857	406	105	5672	.909
2	Philadelphia..	128	75	5011	897	7.00	465	3.62	1654	.330	2168	16.93	355	2.77	3372	1965	465	163	5966	.894
3	Chicago......	125	71	4695	804	6.43	467	3.73	1566	.334	2153	17.22	372	2.97	3336	2164	471	190	6161	.892
4	New York....	129	68	4876	815	6.31	448	3.47	1616	.331	2104	16.31	433	3.28	3335	1982	447	232	5996	.886
5	Boston.......	124	61	4760	808	6.51	412	3.32	1547	.325	2052	16.54	380	3.06	3228	1897	476	162	5693	.887
6	Pittsburg.....	125	55	4735	618	4.94	365	2.92	1462	.306	1845	14.76	211	1.68	3319	1819	432	146	5710	.898
7	Washington...	126	46	4562	601	4.77	316	2.50	1313	.286	1726	13.69	324	2.61	3245	1978	512	210	5945	.878
8	Indianapolis..	127	37	4673	629	4.95	328	2.58	1376	.294	1761	13.89	380	2.59	3251	1904	495	217	5867	.878

TIE GAMES.

Detroit 2, Philadelphia 5, Chicago 4, New York 6, Boston 3, Pittsburg 1, Washington 4, Indianapolis 1.

THE AMERICAN CHAMPIONSHIP SEASON OF 1887.

The American Association championship season of 1887 began on April 16, on which occasion the Brooklyn and Metropolitan teams opened the season at Brooklyn, and the Baltimore and Athletic clubs at Baltimore in the East, while the Louisville and St. Louis teams opened at Louisville, and the Cincinnati and Cleveland teams at Cincinnati in the West, the victorious teams on the occasion being the Brooklyn, Baltimore, Louisville and Cincinnati club teams. At the end of the first week of the campaign Cincinnati led by 5 to 0 in victories and defeats; Brooklyn being second by 3 to 0, and Baltimore third by 3 to 1, the Metropolitan and Cleveland teams alone failing to win at least one game. By the end of April, however, St. Louis had secured the lead with a record of seven victories out of the ten games; Brooklyn being second with six out of eight, and Baltimore third with six out of nine, the Metropolitans standing last on the list without a single victory to their credit out of nine games played. The May campaign still further fixed St. Louis in the position of the coming victors of the campaign; in fact, from the end of April until the finish in October, they were not headed in the pennant race. The close of the May campaign saw St. Louis in the van with a record of 28 victories against but 5 defeats, Baltimore being second with a record of 19 to 12, and the Athletics third with 18 to 14, Brooklyn having fallen back badly, as also Cincinnati, the latter teams having lost more games than they had won up to the close of May. The June campaign ended with the St. Louis champions first in the van, the Baltimore team being second and the Cincinnatis third, the latter having rallied well in June. The Athletics had fallen back badly in the race, while Brooklyn had pulled up. The July running did not materially change the relative position of the contestants, the end of the month leaving St. Louis, Baltimore, and Cincinnati still in the lead, while Louisville had pushed Brooklyn out of fifth place. During the August campaign Louisville made quite a brilliant rally for a leading position in the race, and the result was that the end of the month saw that club's team occupying second place in the race, and Cincinnati third, Baltimore having been driven back to fourth position, and Brooklyn to sixth place. Now came the most exciting month of the campaign, September. The championship question had been virtually settled in St. Louis' favor, but the struggle for second and third positions was still left as the interesting feature of the last quarter's running in the pennant race. Cincinnati began to play a strong up-hill game, and before the month ended that club's team had got into second place, and they remained there. Then followed an interesting contest for third position between Louisville and Baltimore, and between

BASE BALL GUIDE. 69

the Athletic and Brooklyn teams for fifth position. But it was left to October to settle these latter questions, September ending with Louisville third, Baltimore fourth, and Athletic fifth. The ten days' campaign of October enabled Baltimore to drive Louisville back to fourth place, and the Athletics to retain fifth position, the Brooklyns making a bad finish of a season which opened very promisingly for them. The appended monthly records give the complete statistics of the pennant race each month from April 16 to October 10 inclusive.

THE SEASON'S RECORD.

The complete statistical record of the prominent work done by the eight American Association clubs in the championship arena during 1887 is as follows:

	St. Louis.	Cincinnati.	Baltimore.	Louisville.	Athletic.	Brooklyn.	Metropolitan.	Cleveland.	Totals.
Victories........................	95	81	77	76	64	60	44	39	536
Defeats.........................	40	54	58	60	69	74	89	92	536
Games Played.................	135	135	135	136	133	134	133	131	...
Per Cent. of Victories.........	.704	.600	.510	.559	.481	.448	.331	.298	...
Drawn Games.................	3	1	6	3	4	4	5	2	...
Series Won.....................	6	5	5	6	2	2	0	1	...
Series Lost.....................	1	2	2	1	5	4	6	6	...
Series Tied.....................	0	0	0	0	1	1	0	0	...
Victories at Home.............	56	47	43	44	41	36	26	23	316
Victories Abroad...............	39	34	34	32	23	24	18	16	220
Defeats at Home...............	12	26	21	24	27	37	33	40	220
Defeats Abroad................	28	28	37	36	42	37	56	52	316
"Chicago" Victories...........	6	10	7	4	6	3	1	2	39
"Chicago" Defeats............	3	3	2	3	0	6	15	7	39
Victories in Ten Innings Games.	1	1	3	2	1	1	1	0	11
In Eleven " "	1	1	0	0	1	0	0	1	4
In Twelve " "	0	0	0	0	0	0	1	0	1
In Thirteen " "	0	0	0	0	0	1	0	0	1
In Fourteen " "	0	0	1	0	0	0	0	0	1
Double Figure Victories.......	44	28	29	29	25	29	14	14	212
Single Figure Victories........	51	53	48	47	39	31	30	25	324
Double Figure Defeats........	11	19	24	25	22	24	41	48	212
Single Figure Defeats.........	29	35	34	37	47	50	48	44	324
Batting Averages..............	.365	.321	.338	.350	.337	.322	.314	.309	...
Fielding Averages.............	.921	.919	.919	.913	.923	.902	.895	.902	...
Games Won by One Run......	9	13	12	22	13	7	8	10	94
Games Lost by One Run......	8	17	7	12	12	17	9	15	94
Highest Score in Single Game..	28	16	21	27	18	21	18	16	...

MONTHLY RECORDS.

The April campaign in the American Association began on Saturday, the 16th, when the Brooklyns beat the Metropolitans at Brooklyn by 14 to 10; the Baltimores the Athletics at Baltimore by 8 to 3; the Cincinnatis the Clevelands at Cincinnati by 16 to 6, and the Louisvilles the St. Louisians at St. Louis by 8 to 3. Though the champions opened with defeat they led in the race at the end of the month, the Brooklyns being second and the Baltimores third, the record of the month being as follows:

APRIL.

APRIL.	1st wk		2d wk		3d wk		Totals.		
	W.	L.	W.	L.	W.	L.	W.	L.	P.
St. Louis	0	1	2	2	5	0	7	3	10
Brooklyn	1	0	2	0	3	2	6	2	8
Baltimore	1	0	1	1	4	2	6	3	9
Cincinnati	1	0	4	0	1	4	6	4	10
Louisville	1	0	2	2	3	2	6	4	10
Athletic	0	1	2	1	3	1	5	3	8
Cleveland	0	1	0	4	1	4	1	9	10
Metropolitan	0	1	0	3	0	5	0	9	9
Totals	4	4	13	13	20	20	37	37	

The May campaign saw a decided change made in the relative positions of the contesting teams, Louisville working up to second place and the Athletics to third, the Brooklyns falling back from second place in April to sixth position for the May record, St. Louis still having the lead and already being regarded as the coming champions. Here is the May record:

MAY.

MAY.	1st wk		2d wk		3d wk		4th wk		5th wk		Totals.		
	W.	L.	W.	L.	W.	L.	W.	L.	W.	L.	W.	L.	P.
St. Louis	4	0	5	0	5	1	5	1	2	0	21	2	23
Louisville	2	3	3	2	3	3	4	2	1	2	13	12	25
Athletic	2	4	1	3	2	4	6	0	2	1	13	12	25
Baltimore	5	1	0	4	4	2	3	1	1	1	13	9	22
Cincinnati	3	2	4	2	2	4	1	5	1	1	11	14	25
Brooklyn	2	2	3	1	2	4	2	4	0	2	9	13	22
Metropolitan	1	3	1	3	2	3	1	5	1	1	6	15	21
Cleveland	0	4	2	4	3	2	0	4	1	1	6	15	21
Totals	19	19	19	19	23	23	22	22	9	9	92	92	

The month of June saw Baltimore bear off the palm, that club's team winning sixteen out of twenty-one games in June, St. Louis being second and Cincinnati third, Brooklyn having pulled up a little and the Athletics fallen back. The record for the month was as follows:

JUNE.

JUNE.	1st wk		2d wk		3d wk		4th wk		5th wk		Totals.		
	W.	L.	W.	L.	W.	L.	W.	L	W.	L.	W.	L.	P.
Baltimore....	2	1	5	0	2	2	4	1	3	1	16	5	21
St. Louis	3	0	3	3	2	2	4	3	2	1	14	9	23
Cincinnati	2	1	3	3	4	0	4	2	1	4	14	10	24
Brooklyn	1	2	4	2	1	3	3	2	3	1	12	10	22
Louisville	1	1	1	4	2	3	3	2	3	2	10	12	22
Athletic	0	2	3	3	4	2	1	4	1	3	9	14	23
Metropolitan	0	2	3	3	2	3	2	3	1	3	8	14	22
Cleveland	1	1	1	5	2	4	1	5	2	1	7	16	23
Totals	10	10	23	23	19	19	22	22	16	16	90	90	

Louisville did the best in July, that club's team winning seventeen out of twenty-five, St. Louis being second this month and Cincinnati third. The surprise of the month was the fact that the Metropolitans scored as many victories in July as they did defeats. Previously and afterward the defeats were largely in the majority. The record is appended:

JULY.

JULY.	1st wk		2d wk		3d wk		4th wk		5th wk		Totals.		
	W.	L.	W.	L.	W.	L.	W.	L.	W.	L.	W.	L.	P.
Louisville	1	1	5	1	4	2	3	2	4	2	17	8	25
St. Louis	1	1	3	3	5	1	1	1	6	1	16	7	23
Cincinnati	2	0	4	1	6	1	1	3	3	3	16	8	24
Metropolitan	1	1	1	4	2	5	3	0	5	2	12	12	24
Baltimore	1	1	2	3	3	2	2	2	2	5	10	14	24
Brooklyn	1	1	2	2	2	4	3	2	2	6	10	15	25
Athletic	1	1	3	3	0	5	2	1	3	3	9	13	22
Cleveland	0	2	1	4	2	3	0	4	2	5	5	18	23
Totals	8	8	21	21	24	24	15	15	27	27	95	95	

The champions bore off the honors for August, Louisville being second and Cincinnati third, Baltimore falling off badly this month, while the Metropolitans were excelled by the Clevelands. Here is the record;

AUGUST.

AUGUST.	1st wk		2d wk		3d wk		4th wk		5th wk.		Totals.		
	W.	L.	W.	L.	W.	L.	W.	L.	W	L.	W.	L.	P.
St. Louis	3	2	5	1	4	1	5	1	4	0	21	5	36
Louisville	4	1	3	2	2	3	3	2	4	0	16	8	24
Cincinnati	2	3	2	3	4	1	4	2	3	1	15	11	26
Athletic	5	1	0	6	3	2	5	1	0	3	13	13	26
Brooklyn	3	2	5	2	1	5	3	3	0	4	12	16	28
Baltimore	1	4	3	4	3	3	1	5	3	1	11	16	27
Cleveland	2	3	2	5	3	3	2	5	1	2	10	18	28
Metropolitan	1	5	4	1	2	4	1	5	0	4	8	19	27
Totals	21	21	24	24	22	22	24	24	15	15	106	106	

Cincinnati rallied finely in September, and led all the others in the month's record, Baltimore also recovering lost ground, as did the Athletics, the champions doing the poorest of any month of the season in September, as they only won eleven games out of twenty. Brooklyn in this month lost their chance of getting higher than sixth position, they losing nearly two-thirds of the games they played. The record is appended :

SEPTEMBER.

SEPTEMBER.	1st wk		2d wk		3d wk		4th wk		5th wk		Totals.		
	W.	L.	W.	L.	W.	L.	W.	L.	W.	L.	W.	L.	P.
Cincinnati	2	1	4	1	4	1	5	1	1	1	16	5	21
Baltimore	2	0	4	3	2	3	5	1	2	2	15	9	24
Athletic	1	2	2	3	4	1	3	2	2	1	12	9	21
St. Louis	3	0	4	3	3	2	0	3	1	1	11	9	20
Louisville	0	1	4	3	2	2	4	2	0	4	10	12	22
Brooklyn	1	0	3	4	2	3	1	4	1	2	8	13	21
Cleveland	0	2	2	4	2	3	0	3	4	0	8	13	21
Metropolitan	0	3	2	4	1	5	2	4	1	1	6	16	22
Totals	9	9	25	25	20	20	20	20	12	12	86	86	

Baltimore made a bold dash to lead Louisville for third place in the race in October, and succeeded, as will be seen by the appended record :

OCTOBER.

OCTOBER.	1st wk		2d wk		3d wk		Totals.		
	W.	L.	W.	L.	W.	L.	W.	L.	P.
Baltimore	2	0	3	2	1	0	6	2	8
St. Louis	0	1	4	4	1	0	5	5	10
Louisville	1	0	3	3	0	1	4	4	8
Metropolitan	0	0	3	3	1	1	4	4	8
Cincinnati	1	0	1	2	1	0	3	2	5
Athletic	0	2	3	2	0	1	3	5	8
Brooklyn	0	0	2	4	1	1	3	5	8
Cleveland	0	1	2	1	0	1	2	3	5
Totals	4	4	21	21	5	5	30	30	

The complete record of the victories and defeats scored each month from April 16 to October 10 inclusive, is as follows :

FULL RECORD.

	April.		May.		June.		July.		Aug.		Sept.		Oct.		Totals.		
	W.	L.	W.	L.	W.	L.	W.	L.	W.	L.	W.	L.	W.	L.	W.	L.	P.
St. Louis	7	3	21	2	14	9	16	7	21	5	11	9	5	5	95	40	135
Cincinnati	6	4	11	14	14	10	16	8	15	11	16	5	3	2	81	54	135
Baltimore	6	3	13	9	16	5	10	14	11	16	15	9	6	2	77	58	135
Louisville	6	4	13	12	10	12	17	8	16	8	10	12	4	4	76	60	136
Athletic	5	3	13	12	9	14	9	13	13	13	12	9	3	5	64	69	133
Brooklyn	6	2	9	13	12	10	10	15	12	10	8	13	3	5	60	74	134
Metropolit'n	0	9	6	15	8	14	12	12	8	19	6	10	4	4	44	89	133
Cleveland	1	9	6	15	7	16	5	18	10	18	8	13	2	3	39	92	131
Totals	37	37	92	92	90	90	95	95	106	106	86	86	30	30	536	536	

THE SERIES RECORD.

The record of the series of games won, lost and tied by each club in the American championship arena in 1887 is appended. The letters "W" and "L" stand for won and lost.

	St. Louis.	Cincinnati.	Baltimore.	Louisville.	Athletic.	Brooklyn.	Metropolitan.	Cleveland.	Series Won.	Series Lost.	Series Tied.
	W L	W L	W L	W L	W L	W L	W L	W L			
St. Louis.......	....	6-12	16-3	13-7	12-8	16-4	14-5	18-1	6	1	0
Cincinnati.........	12-6	....	9-11	8-12	11-9	13-7	17-3	11-6	5	2	0
Baltimore.........	3-16	11-9	....	7-11	14-5	10-9	15-4	17-3	5	2	0
Louisville.........	7-13	12-8	11-7	....	11-8	12-8	12-8	11-8	6	1	0
Athletic..........	8-12	9-11	6-14	8-11	....	8-10	11-7	14-4	2	5	0
Brooklyn.........	4-16	7-13	9-10	8-12	10-8	....	9-9	13-6	2	4	1
Metropolitan.....	5-14	3-17	4-15	8-12	7-11	9-9	....	8-11	0	6	1
Cleveland....	1-18	6-11	3-17	8-11	4-14	6 13	11-8	....	1	6	0

AMERICAN ASSOCIATION RECORD.

The American championship records for the past six years of the history of the organization are appended as a matter of necessary reference:

RECORD OF 1882.

	Cincinnati.	Athletic.	Eclipse.	Allegheny.	St Louis.	Baltimore.	Won.	Lost.	Played.	Per cent. of Victories.
Cincinnati...............	....	10	11	10	10	14	55	25	80	.68
Athletic............	6	....	11	6	11	7	41	34	75	.54
Eclipse.........	5	5	....	10	9	13	42	38	80	.52
Allegheny........	6	10	6	....	10	7	39	39	79	.50
St. Louis.........	6	5	7	6	....	13	37	43	80	.46
Baltimore.....	2	4	3	7	3	....	19	54	74	.26

RECORD OF 1883.

	Athletic.	St. Louis.	Cincinnati.	Metropolitan.	Louisville.	Columbus.	Allegheny.	Baltimore.	Games Won.	Games Lost.	Games Play'd.	Per cent. of Victories.
Athletic......	....	9	5	9	7	13	12	11	66	32	98	.67
St. Louis...... ..	5	....	6	11	8	11	12	12	65	33	98	.66
Cincinnati	9	8	....	4	10	11	9	11	62	36	98	.64
Metropolitan...... .	5	3	10	....	6	11	9	10	54	42	96	.56
Louisville.....	7	6	4	7	....	9	11	8	52	45	97	.53
Columbus........	1	3	3	3	5	....	10	7	32	65	97	.33
Allegheny	2	2	5	5	3	4	....	9	30	68	98	.30
Baltimore....	3	2	3	3	6	6	5	....	28	68	96	.29

RECORD OF 1884.

	Metropolitan	Columbus	Louisville	St. Louis	Cincinnati	Baltimore	Athletic	Toledo	Brooklyn	Virginia	Pittsburg	Indianapolis	Washington	Games Won	Games Lost	Games Play'd	Per cent. of Victories
Metropolitan.......	..	5	7	5	6	5	8	5	9	2	9	8	6	75	32	107	.700
Columbus...........	4	..	5	5	7	4	5	8	7	2	9	8	5	69	39	108	.638
Louisville..........	3	5	..	5	5	4	6	9	6	4	8	9	4	68	40	108	.629
St. Louis...........	4	5	5	..	6	5	7	5	7	3	9	9	5	67	40	107	.626
Cincinnati..........	4	3	5	4	..	6	4	7	8	4	8	9	6	68	41	109	.623
Baltimore..........	5	6	6	5	4	..	3	5	5	5	9	9	2	63	43	106	.594
Athletic............	2	5	3	3	6	7	..	4	6	2	8	6	7	61	47	108	.564
Toledo.............	4	1	1	5	3	5	3	..	4	4	5	6	5	46	58	104	.442
Brooklyn...........	1	3	3	2	2	5	3	4	..	3	4	7	3	40	64	104	.384
Virginia............	0	2	1	1	0	0	0	0	2	..	4	2	0	12	30	42	.285
Pittsburg...........	1	1	2	1	1	0	2	5	6	1	..	6	4	30	78	108	.277
Indianapolis........	2	2	1	3	1	1	4	3	3	1	4	..	4	29	78	107	.271
Washington........	..	1	1	1	0	1	1	1	1	0	1	2	..	12	51	63	.190

RECORD OF 1885.

	St. Louis	Cincinnati	Pittsburg	Athletic	Brooklyn	Louisville	Metropolitan	Baltimore	Games Won	Games Lost	Games Play'd	Per cent. of Victories
St. Louis...........	..	10	10	12	12	9	12	14	79	33	112	.705
Cincinnati..........	6	..	9	9	11	8	10	10	63	49	112	.562
Pittsburg...........	6	7	..	6	10	10	7	10	56	55	111	.504
Athletic............	4	7	10	..	5	8	11	10	55	57	112	.491
Brooklyn...........	4	5	6	11	..	10	8	9	53	59	112	.473
Louisville..........	7	8	6	8	6	..	9	9	53	59	112	.473
Metropolitan.......	4	6	8	5	8	7	..	6	44	64	108	.407
Baltimore..........	2	6	6	6	7	7	7	..	41	68	109	.376

RECORD OF 1886.

	St. Louis	Pittsburg	Brooklyn	Louisville	Cincinnati	Athletic	Metropolitan	Baltimore	Games Won	Games Lost	Games Play'd	Per cent. of Victories
St. Louis...........	..	12	12	9	15	15	16	13	93	46	139	.669
Pittsburg...........	8	..	12	12	13	11	12	12	80	57	137	.583
Brooklyn...........	7	8	..	13	13	12	10	14	77	61	138	.557
Louisville..........	10	7	7	..	10	9	11	12	66	70	136	.485
Cincinnati..........	5	7	7	10	..	10	13	13	65	73	138	.471
Athletic............	5	8	7	11	10	..	12	10	63	73	136	.463
Metropolitan.......	4	8	9	8	7	8	..	9	53	82	135	.392
Baltimore..........	7	7	7	7	5	8	8	..	48	83	131	.366

BASE BALL GUIDE.

RECORD OF 1887.

	St. Louis.	Cincinnati.	Baltimore.	Louisville.	Athletic.	Brooklyn.	Metropolitan.	Cleveland.	Games Won.	Games Lost.	Games Play'd	Per cent of Victories.
St. Louis........	....	6	16	13	12	16	14	18	95	40	135	.704
Cincinnati........	12	....	9	8	11	13	17	11	81	54	135	.600
Baltimore........	3	11	....	7	14	10	15	17	77	58	135	.570
Louisville........	7	12	11	....	11	12	12	11	76	60	136	.559
Athletic........	8	9	6	8	....	8	11	14	64	69	133	.481
Brooklyn........	4	7	9	8	10	....	9	13	60	74	134	.448
Metropolitan......	5	3	4	8	7	9	....	8	44	89	133	.331
Cleveland........	1	6	3	8	4	6	11	....	39	92	131	.298

THE MINOR LEAGUE RECORDS.

THE NORTHWESTERN LEAGUE.

The Northwestern League was the only one of the minor professional associations of 1887, which was able to go through its scheduled season without the disbandment of a single club. It began with the eight clubs of Oshkosh, Milwaukee, Des Moines, St. Paul, Minneapolis, La Crosse, Duluth and Eau Claire, and these clubs were all in at the finish in October, after a campaign lasting over twenty-three weeks The eight clubs finished in the above named order, leaving the record at the close as follows:

	Oshkosh.	Milwaukee.	Des Moines.	St. Paul.	Minneapolis.	LaCrosse.	Duluth.	Eau Claire.	Won.	Per cent of Victories.
Oshkosh............	....	6	7	12	10	14	12	15	73	.649
Milwaukee.........	11	....	9	6	10	11	17	14	78	.644
DesMoines.........	8	8	....	10	11	11	12	13	73	.619
St. Paul............	6	10	7	....	15	12	13	12	75	.510
Minneapolis........	7	7	6	3	....	11	7	13	54	.453
LaCrosse...........	4	7	7	3	5	....	10	6	45	.365
Duluth.............	3	1	4	5	10	7	....	11	41	.367
Eau Claire.	2	4	5	6	4	12	6	....	39	.317
Lost...............	41	43	45	48	65	78	77	84	481	

INTERNATIONAL LEAGUE.

Next to the Northwestern League came the International League, which only dropped one club. But this League lacked the success which characterized it in 1886. The record of the championship in full is appended:

	Toronto.	Buffalo.	Syracuse.	Newark.	Hamilton.	Jersey City.	Rochester.	Binghamton.	Wilkesbarre.	Scranton.	Won.	Per cent of Victories.
Toronto	....	6	5	8	5	10	8	6	9	8	65	.643
Buffalo	6	...	9	6	6	6	8	4	11	7	63	.611
Syracuse	7	3	....	8	2	8	9	10	8	6	61	.604
Newark	4	6	4	....	7	8	7	5	11	7	59	.602
Hamilton	7	6	9	4	....	6	6	4	7	8	57	575
Jersey City	2	6	4	4	6	....	6	6	10	4	48	.494
Rochester	4	4	3	5	6	6	....	9	5	7	49	.485
Binghamton	1	5	2	2	4	2	1	..	8	2	27	369
Wilkesbarre	3	1	4	1	4	1	4	2	....	6	26	.257
Scranton	2	3	0	1	2	2	3	0	6	....	19	.256
Lost	36	40	40	39	42	49	52	46	75	55	474	

WESTERN LEAGUE.

The Western League had to drop two clubs, but nevertheless had a very lively season in their championship arena, as the appended record shows:

	Topeka.	Lincoln.	Denver.	Leavenworth	Kansas City	Omaha.	Hastings,	St. Joseph.	Emporia.	Wichita.	Won.	Per cent. of Victories.
Topeka	....	10	12	9	15	14	12	11	5	3	83	.775
Lincoln	6	....	11	4	9	13	13	6	0	5	62	.645
Denver	6	7	....	4	7	13	9	5	0	0	51	.510
Leavenworth	3	1	2	....	5	5	3	8	0	0	27	.500
Kansas City	4	6	8	3	....	10	10	8	4	6	49	.480
Omaha	2	4	5	1	8	....	12	6	0	3	36	.356
Hastings	3	3	7	2	5	7	....	6	1	2	33	347
St. Joseph	0	3	4	4	4	3	3	....	0	0	21	.304
Emporia	0	0	0	0	1	0	1	0	....	3	5	....
Wichita	0	1	1	0	0	1	1	0	3	....	7	....
Lost	24	34	49	27	53	65	62	48	13	25	374	

NEW ENGLAND LEAGUE.

The New England League failed to achieve the success in 1887 it attained in 1886, three of the eight clubs with which it started dropping out before the close of the season. There was a close fight at the finish between Lowell and Portland, but the former finally won the pennant, as the appended record shows:

BASE BALL GUIDE. 77

	Lowell.	Portland.	Haverhill Blues.	Manchester.	New Salem.	Lynn.	Haverhill.	Salem.	Won.	Per cent. of Victories.
Lowell............................	....	11	8	8	12	18	7	7	71	.682
Portland..........................	9	....	9	11	10	15	6	8	68	.654
Haverhill Blues................	5	5	....	9	5	8	7	8	47	.566
Manchester.....................	9	6	7	....	10	11	6	6	55	.544
New Salem......................	4	8	7	7	....	7	7	5	45	.473
Lynn...............................	3	3	4	9	11	....	3	7	40	.384
Haverhill.........................	2	3	0	1	1	4	....	4	15	.268
Salem.............................	1	0	1	1	1	1	5	....	10	.181
Lost...............................	33	36	36	46	50	64	41	45	351	

SOUTHERN LEAGUE.

The Southern League's campaign in 1887 was anything but a success, and its failure was largely due to the work of the pool gamblers, who have too long been allowed to bring their pernicious influence to bear on the Southern League Clubs. We are glad to note the fact that Birmingham has taken appeal action to stop pool gambling on base ball grounds this season. Every other Southern League city should follow Birmingham's commendable example. Until they do, honest ball playing will be out of reach in Southern League Club cities. The record of 1887 is as follows :

	New Orleans	Charleston.	Memphis.	Nashville.	Birmingham.	Savannah.	Mobile.	Won.	Per cent. of Victories.
New Orleans.....................	....	11	22	9	20	6	7	75	.652
Charleston........................	17	....	14	9	17	7	2	66	.617
Memphis..........................	13	17	....	5	20	7	4	66	.559
Nashville..........................	6	7	9	....	6	3	3	34	.531
Birmingham.....................	3	4	6	6	..	0	0	19	.230
Savannah.........................	1	1	1	1	0	..	4	8	.228
Mobile.............................	0	1	0	0	0	4	....	5	.200
Lost	40	41	52	30	63	27	20	273	

THE EASTERN LEAGUE.

This League began the season with a schedule containing games arranged for six clubs, viz.: Hartford, New Haven, Springfield, Waterbury, Bridgeport and Danbury, but club after club disbanded, until only the Waterbury and Danbury clubs were left to compete for the pennant, Waterbury finally winning because they staid in the longest and had a better percentage than the Danbury. The record is appended. No official averages were made out:

	Waterbury.	Danbury.	Bridgeport.	Hartford.	New Haven.	Springfield.	Won.	Per cent. of Victories.
Waterbury.................................	....	17	1	8	9	2	37	.493
Danbury....................................	13	....	5	2	7	4	31	.413
Bridgeport.................................	8	9	....	7	7	4	35	.700
Hartford...................................	8	12	4	....	7	4	35	.593
New Hav. n................................	8	6	4	5	....	2	25	.455
Springfield.................................	1	0	1	2	0	....	4	.200
Lost..	38	44	15	24	30	16	167	

THE CALIFORNIA LEAGUE.

We sent for the statistics of this League, but they did not come in time. There were three clubs in the arena, the Pioneers, the Haverley's, and the Greenwood and Morans. The Pioneers won the pennant

EXTRA INNINGS GAMES.

The record of victories and defeats in extra innings games in the American championship arena in 1887 is as follows:

VICTORIES.

Date.	Contesting Clubs.	Cities.	Pitch'rs	Innings	Scores.
June 30	Athletic v. Brooklyn...	Brooklyn...	Atkinson......Porter	13	4- 3
July 7	" v. Cleveland..	Cleveland..	Seward.....Crowell	11	7- 6
May 17	" v. St. Louis...	St. Louis...	Seward .. Carruthers	10	4- 3
May 14	" v. Louisville..	Louisville..	Atkinson.......Neal	10	5- 4
Aug. 17	Baltimore v. Metropol'n	St. George.	Kilroy.... .....Mays	10	2- 1
Sept. 10	" Louisville .	Baltimore..	J. Smith......Hecker	10	3- 2
May 24	" Cincinnati.	Cincinnati..	Kilroy......E. Smith	10	4- 3
Aug. 7	Cincinnati v. Louisville	Louisville..	Smith.... ...Ramsey	11	3- 2
July 16	" v. Metropol'n	St. George..	Serad ....Lynch	10	11-10
May 25	Louisville v. Brooklyn.	Louisville.,	Ramsey.... .. Porter	10	5- 4
June 22	" v. Cleveland.	Cleveland..	Hecker.. Hugh Daily	10	11-10
May 20	Metropol'n v. Louisville	Louisville...	Lynch........Cross	12	9- 8
July 30	" v. Cincinnati	St. George.	Mays.... ...Mullane	10	6- 4
Sept. 11	St. Louis v. Cleveland.	St. Louis...	Foutz.........Gilks	11	9- 7
April 16	Brooklyn v Metropol'n	Brooklyn ..	Porter.... ..Schaeffer	10	11-10
July 15	Cleveland v. Metropol'n	Cleveland..	Morrison.....Lynch	11	7- 6

DRAWN GAMES.

Date.	Contesting Clubs.	Cities.	Pitch'rs		Innings	Scores.
July 19	St. Louis v. Baltimore..	Baltimore	Carruthers..	J. Smith	14	2- 2
July 22	" v. Metropol'n	St. George..	Carruthers..	...Mays	11	2- 2
July 4	Brooklyn v. Cleveland.	Cleveland..	Ferry......	.Morrison	12	7- 7
Sept. 17	Metropol'n v. Athletic.	Philadel'a..	Parsons....	..Seward	10	4- 4

DRAWN GAMES.

The drawn games in the League championship games for 1887 were as follows:

Detroit vs. Washington.. 2—2
Detroit vs. Indianapolis.. 2—2
New York vs. Washington... 3—3
Boston vs. Chicago .... 4—4
New York vs. Chicago.. 5—5
New York vs. Philadelphia .... 5—5
New York vs. Philadelphia .... 5—5
Philadelphia vs. Washington.. 5—5
New York vs. Philadelphia .... 6—6
Boston vs. New York... 6—6
Boston vs. Washington... 7—7
Philadelphia vs. Chicago... 7—7
Chicago vs. Pittsburg.. 7—7

The exhibition games after the championship series were as follows:

EXHIBITION GAMES.

New York vs. Indianapolis... 9—1
Detroit vs. Philadelphia... 9—3
Boston vs. Chicago... 9—4
Boston vs. Chicago... 10—4
Chicago vs. Philadelphia... 10—6

LEAGUE TEAMS OF 1887.

EASTERN TEAMS.

PHILADELPHIA.—*Pitchers*, Ferguson, Daily, Casey, Titcomb, Weyhing, Murphy and Henry. *Catchers*, Clements, Cusick, McGuire, Dallas and Stahling. *Infielders*, Farrar, Bastian, Mulvey and Irwin. *Outfielders*, Wood, Fogarty, Andrews and McCarthy.

NEW YORK.—*Pitchers*. Keefe, Welch, Tiernan, Mattemore and George. *Catchers*, Ewing, O'Rourke, Cuff, Deasley, Brown and Weckbecker. *Infielders*, Connor, Gerhardt, Richardson and Ward. *Outfielders*, Gillespie, Gore and Dorgan.

BOSTON.—*Pitchers*, Radbourne, Stemmyer, Conway, Buffintion and Madden. *Catchers*, Kelly, Daily, Tate, Gunning and O'Rourke. *Infielders*, Morrill, Burdock, Nash and Wise. *Outfielders*, Hornung, Johnston, Poorman, Sutton and Wheelock.

WASHINGTON.—*Pitchers*, Shaw, Gilmore, Whitney, O'Day, and Keating. *Catchers*, Gilligan, Mack, Deally and O'Brien. *Infielders*, Kreig, Farrell, McGlone and Myers. *Outfielders*, Carroll, Hines, Shock, Donnelly, Stuart and Baker.

WESTERN TEAMS.

DETROIT.—*Pitchers*, Baldwin, Getzein, Knowlton, Conway and Smith. *Catchers*, Bennett, Briody, Ganzel and Gillen. *Infielders*, Brouthers, Dunlap, White and Rowe. *Outfielders*, Richardson, Hanlon, Thompson, Manning and Shindle.

CHICAGO.—*Pitchers*, Clarkson, Flynn, Pyle and Baldwin. *Catchers*, Flint, Darling, Daly and Hardee. *Infielders*, Anson, Pfeffer, Williamson and Burns. *Outfielders*, Ryan, Sunday and Sullivan.

PITTSBURG.—*Pitchers*, Galvin, Morris, VanHaltren, Handeboe and Bishop. *Catchers*, Miller, Carroll, Fields and Kuehne. *Infielders*, McKinnon, Berkley, Whitney and Smith. *Outfielders*, Dalrymple, Coleman and Brown.

INDIANAPOLIS.—*Pitchers*, Boyle, Kirby, Healy and Arundel. *Catchers*, Hackett, Graves and Mappes. *Infielders*, Shomberg, Bassett, Denny and Glasscock. *Outfielders*, Seery, McGlachy, Cahill, Quinn and Toohey.

HINTS TO UMPIRES.

INTERPRETING THE NEW RULES.

The experience of each season, in regard to the interpretation given some of the playing rules by umpires and players, shows such a confliction of ideas as to the correct meaning given to many of the sections of the code, that it has come to be a necessity on the part of the editor of the GUIDE to give a chapter each year to the subject of the proper interpreting of every important rule of the game; and we now therefore take up each department of the code of playing rules in order, and give the official interpretation of each rule likely to be misconstrued by either umpires or players.

BATTED BALLS HITTING THE BASES.

Since the first and third bases were placed entirely on fair ground and within the foul lines, every batted ball touching either the first or third base bag must be declared a fair ball, no matter where it strikes after touching either bag. It would be better to have the bags in question on foul ground so as to make every batted ball foul that strikes them; but until this is done, all such batted balls must be declared fair.

COACHERS MUST KEEP WITHIN THEIR LINES.

Captains or their assistants who engage in "coaching" base runners, must keep within the lines of their designated position, or if they attempt to coach a runner while standing outside of their position, they must be fined five dollars for each violation of the rule.

CHANGING A RIPPED BALL.

The umpire is the sole judge of the injury done to the ball by wear and tear, etc., and he alone, can decide whether the ball is in fit condition to be played with, the captains having nothing to do with deciding the question. The ball cannot be changed unless cut or ripped so as to expose the yarn, or so damaged as to be unfit for use, and as to this unfitness for use the umpire is the sole judge.

OPEN BETTING PROHIBITED.

Rule 15 prohibits open betting on all ball grounds of clubs governed by the rules of the *National Agreement*. The penalty for a violation of this rule is the forfeiture of the game which is being played when the rule is violated; and the umpire must enforce this rule or be amenable to a prompt removal from his position.

NO UMPIRE TO BE INSULTED.

The code states that "the umpire is the sole judge of play, and is entitled to the respect of the spectators, and *any person offering any insult or indignity to him must be promptly ejected from the grounds*," under the penalty of a forfeiture of the game.

PLAYERS MUST BE SEATED ON THE BENCH.

Section 2 of Rule 22 requires that the players of the side at the bat, other than the man at the bat and the captain, *must remain seated* on the player's bench until each in his turn is called to the bat. Umpires repeatedly failed to enforce this needed rule last season.

OFFICIAL ORDER OF BATTING.

Section 3 of Rule 22 requires that batsmen must go to the bat "in the order in which they are named an the *score*," and the score referred to is the record of the batting order of the contesting nines kept in the score back of the official scorer of the home club, and has nothing to do with the order printed on the score cards.

DEAD BALLS.

Dead balls include pitched balls which accidentally hit the batsman's bat without being struck at; or which hit any part of the batsman's person, or touch any part of his clothnig while he is standing fairly within the lines of his position. But if he leans over so as to allow any part of his person to be beyond the lines of his position, or purposely stands so as to allow the pitched ball to strike him or touch his person, no dead ball can be declared. If a pitched ball, too, touches the person or clothing of the umpire, before it has been handled by the catcher or passes him, it becomes a dead ball.

CALLED STRIKE.

The new rules for 1888 reduces the number of called strikes from four—as in 1887 to *three;* and when the third strike is called on a batsman, when there is a base runner on first base, the umpire must declare the batsman out whether the ball on the third called strike has been caught by the catcher or not. The batsman is out too,—under the new rule—if, *when the third strike is called, the pitched ball hits him or touches his clothing.* When two hands are out, and there is no base runner on first base, the ball on which the third strike is called must be held by the catcher on the fly, or thrown in time to first base to put the runner out, otherwise he cannot to be declared out on the third strike. In the case of two strikes having been called and the *batsman hits a foul ball with the obvious attempt to do so intentionally,* he must be declared out on three strikes. A strike is defined in Section 3 of Rule 31 as being the result of "any obvious attempt to make a foul hit." The umpire is to judge whether the foul hit ball has been hit intentionally foul or not. If it has than a strike must be called, but not otherwise.

FORFEITED GAMES FROM VIOLATED RULES.

Section 4 of Rule 41 empowers the umpire to declare any game forfeited in which he is personally cognizant of the fact of any single rule having been wilfully violated, the offending team forfeiting the game then and there.

THE UMPIRE SOLE JUDGE OF ILLNESS OR INJURY.

Rule 43 makes the umpire the sole judge as to the nature and extent of the "illness or injury" claimed to disable a player from service on the field. And no substitute can be allowed to take the place of any player of the batting or fielding side in a game, unless in the case of a player disabled from active service in the field or at the bat by such illness or injury as the umpire considers sufficient to render him unfit for play. The captains have nothing to say in the matter. All they can do is to appeal to the Umpire and abide by his decision.

THE CAPTAIN JUDGES THE CONDITION OF THE FIELD.

Whenever rain prevents a game from being commenced, or necessitates its suspension. the captain, and *not the umpire*, is the sole judge as to the ground being in fit condition or not for play to be commenced or resumed.

GAMES TO BEGIN BEFORE SUNSET.

It is now a fixed rule of the game that all contects—regular match games—must be commenced at least *two hours before sunset*. Umpires should notify clubs to this effects during the months of September and October, when contests are apt to begin at an hour too late to enforce this rule. For instance in 1888 the sun sets at 6 P. M. on September 20, and at 5.43 on September 30, and the time is lessened of course each day, and after September 20 games should begin earlier than the accustomed hour of 4 P. M.

SUBSTITUTE IN UNIFORM.

Section 2 of Rule 44 obliges the umpire to insist upon substitute players being in uniform on the grounds ready to take the place of players disabled by injury or illness, as no player not in uniform and ready to act can act as a substitute player.

GAMES STOPPED BY RAIN.

Under Rule 45 the umpire is prohibited from suspending play in a match game on account of rain, unless "*rain falls so heavily that the spectators are compelled, by the severity of the storm*, to seek shelter." If the rain is light, or an ordinary drizzle it is not sufficient to legalize the suspension of a play.

BATTING OUT OF ORDER.

In the case of a batsman taking his position at the bat out of the regular order of batting, as recorded by the official scorer of the home club, the umpire is required to declare him out for so batting out of his turn, unless the error be discovered and the batsman in regular order be placed in position before a fair hit has been made. If this is done, and the regular batsman is substituted, in such case all strikes on called balls charged to the batsman who has batted out of order, must be charged to the batsman whose place he illegally occupied.

BATSMEN CHANGING POSITION.

Last season a custom came into vogue which virtually violated Section 5 of Rule 47. It was the habit some batsmen had of jumping from one batting position to the other just as the pitcher was about to deliver the ball to the bat, this act virtually hindering the catcher from properly fielding the pitched ball. While no rule should prevent a batsman from batting from either the left or the right batting position at his option, it certainly was never intended to allow the change to be made while play was in progress; and it therefore becomes the duty of the Umpire to interpret this rule according to its spirit, and to regard the action of a batsman in jumping from one position to the other as hindering the catcher, and he should declare him out.

BUNTING FOUL BALLS.

In regard to the calling of strikes on "bunted" balls, it has to be said that a number of illegal decisions were made by Umpires last season in calling strikes on "bunted" balls. Section 8 of Rule 47 reads as follows: "The batsman is out—if, after two strikes are called, *he obviously attempts to make a foul hit.*" The punishment inflicted is not for the effort to "bunt" the ball, but for trying to "bunt" it *foul* in order to annoy the pitcher or delay the game. No strikes can legally be called on a batsman who "bunts" a ball fair to the ground, but only when he plainly attempts to "bunt" it foul purposely.

GIVING THE BATSMAN A BASE ON BALKS.

The batsman is not entitled to a base on a balk, except in the case of an *actual delivery* of the ball illegally. In the case of ordinary balks, made without the actual delivery of the ball to the bat, only runners on bases are entitled to take a base. But in the case of a ball delivered by the pitche, after lifting his backward foot before delivery; or after stepping outside of his position in delivery; or after failing to pause before delivery after throwing to a base to put a runner out, in such cases both the batsman and the base runner are entitled to a base on the balk, because the balk is that of "an illegal delivery."

PASSED BALLS WHICH GIVE A BASE.

In the case of a pitched ball which passes the catcher and then touches the Umpire; or if such passed ball touches any fence or building within ninety feet of the home base, the runner is entitled to one base without being put out, and can of course take more at his own risk.

OBSTRUCTING BASE RUNNERS.

Section 5 of Rule 50 has been, in one sense, a dead letter rule of the game for years. It states that the base-runner shall be entitled to a base every time that he *is prevented from making a base by the obstruction of an adversary.* There is scarcely a game played in which base runners are not prevented from making a base by the obstruction of a fielder. It is invariably done when the fielder stands in front of the base and the base runner collides with him in his effort to make the base. But the obstruction named in the section and that intended as the spirit of the rule, are two different things. It is not a legal obstruction when the fielder, with ball in hand, stands ready to touch the advancing runner, but only when he stands in his way before holding the ball. Umpires should bear in mind this distinction. The rule needs revision in its wording.

BASE BALL GUIDE. 85

THE CAPTAIN ONLY CAN ADDRESS THE UMPIRE.

Rule 58 is explicit in prohibiting any player, except the captain of the nine, from addressing the Umpire in regard to any decision he may make ; and even the captain can only do so in the case of a question involving an error in misinterpreting the rules. If the decision disputed involves only an error of judgment, even the captain has no right to question the decision In every case of a violation of this rule, the Umpire must fine the offender *five dollars*, or he himself be liable to immediate dismissal for violating the rules.

THE UMPIRE'S POWER.

Under Section 3 of Rule 61, the Umpire *is invested with the authority to order any player to do, or to omit to do, any act, as he may deem it necessary*, to give force or effect to any or all of the provisions of the code of playing rules. He is empowered to inflict a fine of from five to twenty-five dollars for each and every refusal of a player to obey his legal commands in this respect. This gives him the authority to decide all disputed points in a game not expressly covered by the rules, subject, of course, to legal protest.

A BATTED BALL STRIKING A BASE RUNNER.

Section 12 of Rule 53 has been reworded so as to decide a base runner out who is hit by a batted ball, only when such ball strikes him before touching a fielder. The intention in revising this section was to have exempted the runner from being put out from being struck by a batted ball in all cases where the batted ball would otherwise have been a base hit, but it does not do so. For instance, if the batted ball touches a fielder first and then glances off and hits the runner, then the runner cannot be decided out ; but if the ball is hit so as to be sent clear of the reach of an infielder—as in the case of a clean base hit—and it then strikes the runner, the latter must be decided out. This is not fair to the runner.

BALL HELD BY PITCHER IN POSITION.

The cases in which a batted ball must be held by the pitcher while standing in his position, before it can be legally in play, are in the case of a *foul strike;* a *foul hit* ball not caught flying ; a *dead ball;* a *block*, or in the case of a batted ball striking a runner which puts him out. In all these cases the ball must be fielded to the pitcher and the latter have held it while standing in his box before it can be put in play.

INTERFERENCE WITH THROWN BALL.

No base runner can legally interfere with a fielder attempting to field a batted ball. The runner has no right to the line of the base when a fielder is occupying it in the effort to catch a fly ball, or to field a batted ball ; nor can a base runner make any attempt to hinder or obstruct a fielder from fielding a thrown ball without his being promptly decided out. In all cases the base runner must run off the line of the bases to avoid interfering with a fielder standing on the line of the bases to field a batted ball. Section 8 of Rule 53 says, "*or intentionally interferes with a thrown ball,*" and the intention is judged by his effort to avoid interference or not.

OVERRUNNING FIRST BASE.

The base runner, in running to first base, is only exempt from being touched out after overruning the base, when he turns to the right after overrunning the base. If he crosses the foul line after overrunning, toward second base, that is tantamount to turning to the left, but so long as he is on foul ground after overrunning the base, it is immaterial whether he turns to the left or the right. The leaving foul ground in overrunning decides the point against him. It is best, however, always to turn to the right in returning.

NO SUBSTITUTE FOR BASE RUNNERS.

The Umpire must bear in mind that Rule 52 expressly prohibits any player being substituted for a base runner, whether by consent of the two captains or not. If a runner be disabled he must leave the nine and have a substitute player take his place under the clause granting a substitute in case of illness or injury. But no one player in the nine can run a base for another player who is the base runner under the rules.

DOUBTFUL DECISIONS IN FAVOR OF THE BATTING SIDE.

The rules expressly make a distinction in favor of the batting side in all cases where there is any doubt as to the player being fairly out. Especially is this the case in the case of the batsman's being put out at first base, for Section 5 of Rule 53 requires the ball to be securely held by the base player "*before*" the runner touches the base in order to put him out, and the rule applies to the touching out of all base runners on bases ; the words being "*before*" the runner reaches the base. If at the same time, he—the runner—is not out. Time and again were base runners unfairly decided out last season in cases where the ball was held by the base player simultaneously with the runner's touching the base, every such decision being illegal.

THE EASTERN TEAMS IN CALIFORNIA.

Through the courtesy of the able base ball editor of the California *Spirit of the Times*, Mr. Walter Wallace, we are enabled to give our base ball readers the official record of the games played by the New York, St. Louis, Chicago and Philadelphia picked nines which visited San Francisco last November. In all twenty first-class matches were played by the visiting teams with the three club teams of the California League during November, December and January, the home teams at times being aided by visiting players. There were eight games played on the Central Park grounds, and twelve on the California League grounds as follows:

PLAYED AT THE CENTRAL PARK GROUNDS.

DATE.	CONTESTING CLUBS.	PITCHERS.	SCORE.
Nov. 19,	Chicago vs. Philadelphia	Mullane and Crane	12—3
" 26,	" " "	Ryan and Crane	10—2
" 27,	St. Louis vs. Chicago	King and Mullane	16—9
Dec. 10,	Chicago vs. Philadelphia	Mullane and Viau	9—6
" 11,	" " "	Ryan and Crane	15—8
" 25,	St. Louis vs. Chicago	Foutz and Ryan	11—3
" 26,	" " " "	King and Mullane	17—3
" 31,	Philadelphia vs. St. Louis	Crane and Foutz	6—0

PLAYED AT THE CALIFORNIA LEAGUE GROUNDS.

Nov. 19, A. M.	New York vs. Haverleys	Keefe and Incell	9—2
" 19, P. M.	G. and M. vs. New York	Van Haltren and Keefe	10—4
" 26,	New York vs. Pioneers	Keefe and Lorrigan	1—0
Dec. 3,	" " "	G. and M. Ewing and Boarchers	17—3
" 10,	" " "	Pioneers Ewing and Purcell	11—1
" 11,	" " "	Haverleys Keefe and Meegan	8—0
" 24,	Pioneers vs. New York	Muller and Ewing	16—8
" 25,	G. and M. vs. New York	Boarchers and Keefe	14—7
Jan. 7,	St. Louis vs. Haverleys	Foutz and Incell	14—6
" 14,	" " "	Pioneers Foutz and Purcell	5—3
" 8,	" " "	New York King and Van Haltren	1—0
" 15,	New York vs. St. Louis	Van Haltren and King	5—0

Not a hit was made off VanHaltern's pitching in this game.

THE COLLEGE CLUB STATISTICS.

THE COLLEGE LEAGUE.

The Eastern College League in 1887 was organized with but four clubs, viz.: Those of Harvard, Yale and Princeton, with their "university nines," and Columbia. The latter failed to meet its engagements after May, and its games were thrown out. The season's record of championship games is appended:

April 30,	Harvard vs. Columbia, at New York	12- 0
" 30,	Yale vs. Princeton, at Princeton	2- 1
May 4,	Princeton vs. Columbia, at Princeton	12- 4
" 9,	Harvard vs. Princeton, at Princeton	3- 1
" 14,	Princeton vs. Columbia, at New York	24- 2
" 14,	Yale vs. Harvard, at New Haven	14- 2
" 21,	Yale vs. Columbia, at New York	20- 1
" 21,	Harvard vs. Princeton, at Princeton	18-11
" 28,	Princeton vs. Harvard, at Cambridge (10 innings)	11-10
June 4,	Yale vs. Princeton, at New Haven	15- 0
" 8,	Harvard vs. Yale, at Cambridge	7- 5
" 11,	Yale vs. Princeton at Princeton	9- 3
" 18,	Yale vs. Princeton, at New Haven	10- 4
" 25,	Yale vs. Harvard, at Cambridge (13 innings)	5- 4
" 28,	Yale vs. Harvard, at New Haven	6- 3

The full record is appended:

	Yale.	Harvard.	Princeton.	Columbia.	Won.	Per cent of Victories
Yale..................	......	14-2 5-4 6-3	2-1 15-0 9-3 10-4	20-1	8	......
Harvard...............	7-5	......	3-1 18-11	12-0	4	......
Princeton..............	0	11-10	......	12-4 24-2	3	......
Columbia..............	0	0	0	......	0	......
Lost..................	1	4	6	4	15	

The Columbia games were not counted in the championship record.

THE AVERAGES FOR 1887.

We are indebted to Mr. Stagg, Yale's most effective pitcher, for the records given below. He sent us in the full table, but the only figures of any use are those given in the appended table:

PLAYERS.	Position.	No. of Games.	Average B. H.	Fielding Average.
McConkey, Yale............	2d b	7	346	950
Willard, Harvard...........	1st b	7	333	974
Hunt, Yale.................	c f	8	324	800
Stagg, Yale................	p	8	307	929
Campbell, Harvard.........	4 c 3 3d b	7	303	796 750
Kellogg, Yale..............	5 r f 3 l f	8	297	1000 000
Noyes, Yale................	s s	8	289	800
Henshaw, Harvard.........	3 c 1 r f	4	263	886 0
Reynolds, Princeton........	l f	6	261	929

BASE BALL GUIDE.   89

THE AVERAGES FOR 1887.—CONTINUED.

Players.	Position.	No. of Games.	Average B. H.	Fielding Average.
Stewart, Yale	1 2d b / 6 3d b	7	261	1000 / 904
Durell, Princeton	r f	5	235	750
Cross, Yale	2 3d b / 2 l f	4	235	666 / 666
Spencer, Yale	1st b	8	228	969
Mercur, Princeton	p	6	227	748
Wagenhurst, Princeton	3d b	7	227	762
Mumford, Harvard	2d b	7	200	838
Brownlee, Princeton	c	6	190	782
Boyden, Harvard	4 p / 3 c f	7	185	775 / 857
Foster, Harvard	l f	7	182	1000
Duffield, Princeton	3 r f / 1 2d b	4	176	1000 / 800
Wiestling, Harvard	s s	7	161	733
Bingham, Harvard	3 p / 4 c f	7	156	957 / 750
Larkin, Princeton	1st b	7	148	975
Price, Princeton	s s	7	143	643
Dann, Yale	c	8	121	960
Evans, Princeton	c f	6	115	812
Linn, Harvard	2 2d b / 5 r f / 1 l f	7	107	500 / 500 / 750
King, Princeton	5 3d b / 1 p	7	77	913 / 1000
PLAYED IN LESS THAN FOUR GAMES.				
Brigham, Yale	l f	3	357	633
McClintock, Yale	r f	3	100	1000
Holden, Harvard	3d b	2	0	700
McCance, Princeton	2d b	1	500	1000
Ford, Princeton	c	1	0	1000
Morgan, Harvard	r f	1	0	0

SCHEDULE OF COLLEGE SEASON FOR 1888.

April 28, Yale vs. Princeton at Princeton.
May 5, Yale vs. Princeton at New Haven.
May 7, Princeton vs. Harvard at Cambridge.
May 12, Harvard vs. Princeton at Princeton.
May 19, Harvard vs. Yale at New Haven.
May 26, Princeton vs. Yale at Princeton.
May 30, Harvard vs. Princeton at Princeton.
June 2, Harvard vs. Princeton at Cambridge.
June 9, Harvard vs. Yale at Cambridge.
June 16, Princeton vs. Yale at New Haven.
June 23, Harvard vs. Yale at Cambridge.
June 26, Harvard vs. Yale at New Haven.

THE AMERICAN COLLEGE ASSOCIATION.

The representatives of the Colleges comprising the American College Base Ball Association assembled in convention in the parlors of the Massasoit House, at Springfield, Mass., on Friday, March 9, 1887.

The meeting was called to order by Vice-President White, and delegates from Amherst, Brown, Williams and Yale were found to be present.

According to the conditions upon which Williams was admitted in 1886, she was obliged to withdraw, and Dartmouth took her old place in the League.

Reports for the preceding year were then read and accepted.

The resignations of Harvard, Princeton and Yale were presented and accepted, and Williams re-admitted, thus making the Association for 1887 to consist of Amherst, Brown, Dartmouth and Williams.

The following officers were elected :

President—F. D. White, of Brown.

Vice-Presidents—Bryant Smith, of Amherst ; Chas. D. Cooke, of Brown.

Secretary and Treasurer—W. H. Dartt, of Dartmouth.

Judiciary Committee—F. D. White, of Brown, ex-officio ; P. C. Phillips, of Amherst ; C. D. Cooke, of Brown ; A. Quackenboss, of Dartmouth ; Henry Burden, 2d, of Williams.

The usual routine of business was then taken up and disposed of. The playing rules of the preceding year were adopted with a few changes, and it was voted that the "Spalding" ball be used by the Association for the next three (3) years. The schedule of games for the season was made out and adopted, and the Convention adjourned till the second Friday of March, 1888.

The following is the schedule of games, with scores, as played by the clubs, season of 1887 :

May 3,	Amherst vs. Brown, at Amherst	14— 1
" 4,	" " " " "	14— 4
" 6,	Williams vs. Dartmouth, at Williamstown	7— 6
" 7,	" " " " "	4— 3
" 11,	Williams vs. Amherst, at Amherst	10— 2
" 11,	Dartmouth vs. Brown, at Providence	31—16
" 12,	" " " " "	25— 8
" 18,	Dartmouth vs. Amherst, at Hanover	13— 1
" 19,	" " " " "	26— 7
" 20,	Williams vs. Brown, at Providence	14— 3
" 21,	" " " " "	2— 2
" 30,	Williams vs. Amherst, at Williamstown	5— 3
June 8,	Dartmouth vs. Williams, at Hanover	5— 4
" 9,	" " " " "	8— 7
" 14,	Dartmouth vs. Amherst, at Amherst	21— 7
" 15,	" " " " "	14—12
" 17,	Williams vs. Brown, at Williamstown	30— 3
" 18,	" " " " "	23— 7
" 20,	Amherst vs. Brown, at Springfield	23— 5
" 22,	" " Williams, at Williamstown	6— 3
" 27,	" " " " Amherst	9— 7

The following is the record in full :

COLLEGE ASSOCIATION, 1887.	Dartmouth.	Williams.	Amherst.	Brown.	Won.	Per cent. of Victories.
Dartmouth.................................	......	5-4 8-7	13-1 26-7 21-7 14-12	31-12 25-8 9-0 9-0	10	.833
Williams...................................	7-6 4-3	......	10-6 5-3	14-3 24-2 30-3 23-7	8	.667
Amherst...................................	0	6-3 9-7	......	14-1 14-4 23-5	5	.455
Brown.....................................	0	0	0	......	0	.000
Lost.......................................	2	4	6	11	23	

THE AVERAGES.

The averages of the American College Association for 1887 are appended. Only the batting and fielding averages were sent in, these not including the names of the positions of the players in the field :

Batting Rank	NAME.	No. Games.	Stolen Bases.	Batting Av.	Fielding Av.
1	Turner, A....................................	10	10	.437	.853
2	Keay, D.....................................	10	12	.417	.785
3	Wilson, W...................................	12	9	.408	.950
4	Dascomb, D..................................	10	11	.404	.781
5	Warren, B....................................	7	5	.400	.692
6	Alvord, A....................................	11	3	.384	.909
7	Johnson, D...................................	5	3	.375	.983
8	Duryea, W...................................	12	10	.370	.862
9	Storrs, A....................................	11	5	.358	.777
10	W. A. Brown, W.............................	6	5	.357	.900
11	Quackenboss, D.............................	10	14	.347	.853
12	Judson, A...................................	10	12	.342	.904
13	Ranlett, D...................................	11	5	.333	.800
14	Clark, W....................................	12	7	.327	.944
15	W. Perry, W.................................	12	6	.321	.920
16	Aiken, D.....................................	10	5	.315	.830
17	Belcher, A...................................	5	1	.313	.786

THE AVERAGES.—CONTINUED.

18 Benden, W.	9	6	.300 .931
19 Blackington, W.	10	7	.298 .738
20 Scruton, D.	10	5	.294 .98
21 Chandler, D.	10	0	.283 .989
21 Campbell, W.	12	10	.283 .782
22 Howey, B.	8	0	.281 .818
23 Norton, D.	10	5	.271 .645
24 O. S. Brown, W.	9	5	.243 .807
25 Nape, A.	9	1	.237 .819
25 Quick, B.	9	3	.237 .774
26 McLennon, A.	7	5	.226 .821
27 Phillips, A.	11	5	.219 .816
28 Artz, D.	5	2	.217 .940
29 Stearns, A.	8	9	.212 .830
30 Van Wormer, W.	12	6	.204 .833
31 Hawthorne, B.	7	1	.190 .580
32 Cooke, B.	6	1	.182 .865
33 Davidson, A.	10	2	.131 .991
34 Blaisdell, B.	6	2	.130 .692
35 Murphy, B.	5	2	.118 .617
36 Brownell, B.	9	0	.107 .918
37 McKenzie, B.	6	0	.095 .714

Those who took part in less than five games averaged as follows:

Batting Rank.	NAME.	No. Games.	Stolen Bases.	Batting Av.	Fielding Av.
1	C. Perry, W.	2	0	333	1.000
2	Oldham, A.	4	0	.286	.666
3	Dickerman, A.	3	2	.231	.143
4	Johnson, B.	3	0	.182	.583
5	Rathburne, B.	3	0	.090	.791
6	Hunter, B.	4	1	.077	.941

CONVENTION OF THE AMERICAN COLLEGE B. B. A.

On Feb. 15, 1888, ex-Captain Quackenboss of Dartmouth, called the second annual Collegiate Base Ball Convention to order in the private parlors of the Massasoit House, Springfield. Dartmouth was represented by Messrs. Fairbanks, Keay, Moulton, White and Quackenboss; Williams by Manager Newell and

Clark; Brown by Hall and Williams, and Amherst by Wilkinson, Tenney and Storrs. R. N. Fairbanks was elected president; A. F. Clark first vice-president; G. D. Storrs, second vice-president, and H. L. Wilkinson, secretary and treasurer. The business of last year was discussed and finished. Brown presented her resignation, which was accepted. The petition of Trinity for admission was then presented and it was voted to allow Messrs. Morgan and Brinley to present her claims. After discussion Trinity was admitted as the fourth member of the Association. The National League rules were adopted with such exceptions as the judiciary committee should recommend. The constitution was amended so that the annual meeting should take place in Springfield on the second Wednesday of February at 10 A. M. instead of on the second Friday of March. The judiciary committee consisting of Captains Clark, Keay, Storrs and Brinley, recommended that the rule "that a batter hit by pitched ball be given his base" should not be adopted. They then adopted the following schedule, and at 5 P. M. the Convention adjourned :

May 4 and 5, Dartmouth vs. Amherst, at Amherst.
" 4 and 5, Trinity vs. Williams, at Williamstown.
" 9, Amherst vs. Williams, at Amherst.
" 9 and 10, Trinity vs. Dartmouth, at Hanover.
" 15 and 16, Williams vs. Dartmouth, at Hanover.
" 18 and 19, Williams vs. Trinity, at Hartford.
" 22 and 23, Dartmouth vs. Trinity, at Hartford.
" 23 Amherst vs. Williams, at Williamstown.
" 29 and 30, Amherst vs. Trinity, at Hartford.
" 29 and 30, Dartmouth vs. Williams, at Williamstown.
June 6, Amherst vs. Williams, at Amherst.
" 9, Amherst vs. Williams, at Williamstown,
" 15 and 16, Amherst vs. Dartmouth, at Hanover.
" 23 and 25, Amherst vs. Trinity, at Amherst.

INTER-COLLEGIATE GAMES OF MICHIGAN.

The Inter-Collegiate Association was formed in 1886, when Albion College, at her annual field day (June 3) offered a championship belt to the college that could hold it two years. The University of Michigan was barred out of the contest, but entered into the games in 1887 with the champions. The following is the record of the games for 1887:

RECORD FOR 1887.

The following are the games as played:

April 29, M. A. C. vs. University, at Agricultural College.......... 9—8
May 13, Albion vs. Olivet, at Olivet............................ 13—6
" 14, M. A. C. vs. Olivet, at Olivet, (5 innings) .... 8—2
" 27, Albion vs. M. A. C., at Albion............................ 9—7
June 3, M. A. C. vs. Olivet, at Agricultural College............ 8—0
" 4, M. A. C. vs. Albion, at Agricultural College.............. 21—8
" 11, M. A. C. vs. University, at Ann Arbor.................... 11—9
May 20, Olivet vs. Albion, at Albion (No record)................

The record in full is as follows:

	M. A. C.	Albion.	Olivet.	Ann Arbor.	Won.	Per cent. of Victories.
M. A. C.		21–8	8–2 8–0 13–6	9–8 11–9 0	5	.833
Albion	9–7		no rec.	0	2	.500
Olivet	0			0	1	.250
Ann Arbor	0		0		0	.000
Lost	0	2	3	2		

The following is the record of the players arranged alphabetically. The record for the Albion and Olivet players will probably vary some from these figures as no record was kept of one game.

BATTING AND FIELDING AVERAGES.

NAME.	CLUB.	Games pla'ed.	Per cent. Batting.	Per cent. Fielding.
Bailey, 1 b	Ann Arbor	1	.400	.818
Bates, lf and c	M. A. C	6	.379	.742
Bistle, ss	Olivet	3	.111	.714
Booth, c and lf	Ann Arbor	1	.250	1.000
Bulson, 2b	M. A. C	6	.435	.666
Canfield, 1 b, 3 b, p	"	5	.292	.842
Carpenter, ss, 2b	Ann Arbor	2	.200	.666
Catton, 2b	Olivet	1	.250	.625
Chase, cf, c	M. A. C	6	.321	.800
Cordly, rf	"	5	.409	1.000
Dascom, 3 b	Albion	3	.357	.384
Douglas, rf, 3b	Olivet	2	.000	.333
Eslow, c	Albion	3	.466	.933
Furber, 2 b, rf	Olivet	3	.200	1.000
Gage, c	"	3	.250	1.000
Gale, 3 b	Ann Arbor	1	.250	.500
Hibbard, p, lf	"	2	.300	.833
Hoskins, p	Olivet	3	.222	.945
Jaycox, rf	Ann Arbor	1	.500	1.000
Jones, p	Albion	3	.500	.976
Joiner, 1 b	Olivet	3	.363	.928
Kester, 3 b	"	1	.500	.500
Kellogg, lf	"	3	.000	1.000

BASE BALL GUIDE. 95

BATTING AND FIELDING AVERAGES.—CONTINUED.

Knappen, lf................................	Albion.......	3	.071	.750
Landon, 2 b................................	"	3	.241	.784
Lawson, rf.................................	Ann Arbor...	1	.400	1.000
Learned, 1 b, rf...........................	M. A. C.....	3	.363	888
Malley, cf.................................	Ann Arbor...	1	.400	1.000
McDonald, c, lf............................	" ...	2	.100	1.000
McMillan, 2 b, p...........................	" ...	2	.500	.833
Miller, 3 b, c..............................	" ...	2	.600	.900
McCulloch, 3 b.............................	M. A. C.....	4	.333	.416
Moore, cf..................................	Olivet.......	2	.000	.000
Shepard, ss................................	M. A. C.....	5	.150	.920
Smith, lf, cf, c............................	"	6	.321	.700
Sherk, cf..................................	Olivet.......	1	.000	1.000
Snell, rf...................................	Albion.......	3	.143	1.000
Sutton, 1 b................................	"	3	.214	.884
Titman, cf.................................	"	2	.222	1.000
Tyler, rf...................................	Olivet.......	1	.500	1.000
Wilkinson, 1 b and f.......................	Ann Arbor...	2	.500	1.000
Yerkes, p, 1 b..............................	M. A. C.....	6	.461	1.000

The following is the record of the pitchers in the season's games.

PITCHERS' RECORD IN ALPHABETICAL ORDER.

		Games.	R. E. by Opponents.	B. H. made by Opponents.	Per cent. of Hits made by Oppon'nts.	Wild Pitches.	B. B. to Opponents.	Per cent. Fielding.
Canfield...............	M. A. C......	1	0	3	.091	0	0	.923
Hibbard	Ann Arbor...	1	6	15	.384	0	2	1.000
Hoskins	Olivet........	3	15	31	.215	2	2	.900
Jones..................	Albion........	3	21	44	.336	1	9	.953
McMillan..............	Ann Arbor...	1	5	15	.349	3	3	.666
Yerkes.................	M. A. C......	5	13	53	.224	0	13	1.000

THE NEW YORK STATE INTER-COLLEGIATE BASE BALL LEAGUE.

This League has been in existence since 1882, but was reformed and placed under its present constitution and by-laws in 1884, since which time men who were not in regular attendance at the college or university which they represented were barred from playing. This prevented the composition of a nine of three or four strictly college men, and the balance of substitutes hired for the occasion. In 1885 the Association was composed of Cornell University, Hamilton College, Hobart College, Syracuse University, Rochester University and Union College. Cornell carried off the championship pennant of that year. In 1886 Rochester University was not in the Association. Cornell again carried off the pennant. In 1887, Cornell withdrew and Rochester re-entered, when Hobart took the first pennant, and Sycamore took second. The following is the summary of games:

	Hobart.	Syracuse.	Rochester.	Hamilton.	Union.	Won.	Per cent. of Victories.
Hobart..........................	....	1	2	2	2	7	.875
Syracuse........................	1	....	1	1	2	5	.625
Rochester.......................	0	1	....	1	1	3	.375
Hamilton........................	0	1	1	....	1	3	.375
Union...........................	0	0	1	1	....	2	.250
Lost............................	1	3	5	5	6	20	

The general averages of the Association were not sent in.

THE REPORTERS' NATIONAL ASSOCIATION.

An event in the history of the game for 1887, was the organization of *The Base Ball Reporters' Association of America*, which took place at the Grand Hotel, Cincinnati, on December 9, 1887, on which occasion representatives of daily and weekly papers which devote special space to base ball, were present from New York and Philadelphia in the East, and Cincinnati, St. Louis and Cleveland in the West. The officers chosen on the occasion to serve until the first annual meeting to be held in St. Louis in December, 1888, were as follows:

George Munson, President, St. Louis *Sporting News*.
Henry Chadwick, Vice-President, New York *Clipper*.
Geo. E. Stackhouse, Secretary, New York *Tribune*.
John H. Mandigo, Treasurer, New York *Sun*.

BOARD OF DIRECTORS.

Joe Pritchard, St. Louis ————; Ren. Mulford, Jr., Cincinnati *Times-Star*; Frank H. Brunell, F. C. Richter, Philadelphia *Sporting Life*.

COMMITTEE ON ORGANIZATION.

J. C. Kennedy, New York *Sporting Times;* Henry Chadwick, F. H. Brunell, Cleveland *Plain Dealer*.

At this meeting Managers Schmelz of the Cincinnati Club; Williams of the Cleveland, and Watkins of the Detroit, were present and aided in the organization of the association, and in the discussion on the amendments proposed for the scoring rules of the national code of playing rules. A committee of the new Association was delegated to attend the American Association convention, and they were cordially received and the new organization highly approved of by the comvention delegates. The following constitution was adopted:

CONSTITUTION OF THE REPORTERS' BASE BALL ASSOCIATION OF AMERICA.

This organization shall be known as the Base Ball Reporters' Association of America.

OBJECTS.

The objects of this Association shall be to promote the welfare of the National Game, and to bring about a thorough and regular system of base ball scoring, on which to base reliable statistics for the use of the National League and the American Association, from which their annual averages can be correctly made up.

MEMBERSHIP.

All regular base ball reporters in good standing shall be eligible to membership of this association on the payment of the annual dues.

OFFICERS.

The officers of this association shall be a President, Vice-President, Secretary, Treasurer, and a Board of five Directors, the same to hold office for one year, or until their successors are elected.

DUTIES OF OFFICERS.

The duties of the President shall be to preside at all meetings of the association, appoint all committees not chosen by the special vote of the association, and to perform all other such duties as pertain to his position. He shall act as ex-officio member of the Board of Directors. The duties of the Vice-President shall be to perform all duties of the President in his absence.

The duties of the Secretary shall be to take charge of all books and documents of the association, attend to necessary correspondence, and such other duties as the Board of Directors may require.

The Treasurer's duty shall be to take charge of all the funds of the association received by him from the Secretary and other officers of the Association.

The Board of Directors shall act as the executive committee in the transaction of the business affairs of the association.

DUES.

The annual dues of this association shall be $1, payable in advance on presentation of nomination for election.

AMENDMENTS.

Amendments to the constitution of this association can only be made at the annual meeting. No change in the constitution and by-laws can be made unless by a two-thirds vote of a total quorum of the members present.

QUORUM.

A legal quorum of any meeting of this association shall be a majority of the officers of the association.

THE NATIONAL AGREEMENT OF PROFESSIONAL BASE BALL CLUBS.

THIS AGREEMENT, made between the Association known and designated as the National League of Professional Base Bal Clubs of the one part, and the Association known and designated as the American Association of Base Ball Clubs, of the other part, witnesseth, that :

I. This document shall be entitled The National Agreement, and shall supersede and be a substitute for all other Agreements, similarly or otherwise designated, heretofore existing between the parties hereto.

II. *a.* No contract shall be made for the services of any player by any Club member of either party hereto for a longer period than seven months, beginning April 1st, and terminating October 31st, and no such contract for services to be rendered after the expiration of the current year shall be made prior to the 20th day of October of such year, nor shall any player enter into any negotiation or contract with any Club, Club agent, or individual for services to be rendered in an ensuing year prior to the said 20th of October. Upon written proofs of a violation of this section the Board of Arbitration shall disqualify such player for and during said ensuing year, and shall inflict a fine of five hundred dollars, payable forthwith into the treasury of the Board, upon the Club in whose interest such negotiations or contract was entered into.

b. Every regular contract shall be forwarded within ten days after its execution to the Secretary of the Association of which the contracting Club is a member, for registry and approval, who shall forthwith notify the Secretary of the other Association party hereto, and the other Club members of his Association.

III. When a player under contract with or reservation by any Club member of either Association party hereto is expelled, blacklisted, suspended, or rendered ineligible in accordance with its rules, notice of such disqualification shall be served upon the Secretary of this Board by the Secretary of the Association from whose Club such player shall have been thus disqualified, and the Secretary of this Board shall forthwith serve notice of such disqualification upon the Secretary of the other Association party hereto. When a player becomes ineligible under the provisions of this Agreement, the Secretary of this Board shall notify the Secretaries of the Associations parties hereto of such disqualification, and from the receipt of such notice all Club members of the parties hereto shall be debarred from employing or playing with, or against, such disqualified player, until the period of disqualification shall have terminated, or the disqualification be revoked by the Association from which such player was disqualified, or by this Board, and due notice of such revocation served upon the Secretary of the other Association, and by him upon his respective Clubs.

IV. On the tenth day of October in each year the Secretary of each Association shall transmit to the Secretary of the other Association a reserve list of players, not exceeding fourteen in number, then under contract with each of its several Club members, and of such players reserved in any prior annual reserve list, who have refused to contract with said Club members and of all other ineligible players, and such players, together with all others thereafter to be regularly contracted with by such Club members, are and shall be ineligible to contract with any Club member of the other Association, except as hereinafter prescribed.

V. Upon the release of a player from contract or reservation with any Club member of either Association party hereto, the services of such player shall at once be subject to the acceptance of the other Clubs of such Association, expressed in writing or by telegraph, to the Secretary thereof for a period of ten days after notice of said release, and thereafter if said services be not so accepted, said player may negotiate and contract with any other Club. The Secretary of such Association shall send notice to the Secretary of the other Association of said player's release on the date thereof, and of said acceptance of his services at or before the expiration of the ten days aforesaid.

VI. No Club not a member of either Association party hereto shall be entitled to membership in either Association party hereto from any city or town in which any Club member of either Association party hereto is located. *Provided* that nothing herein contained shall prohibit any Club member of either Association party hereto from resigning its membership in such Association during the month of November in any year, and being admitted to membership in the other Association, with all rights and privileges conferred by this agreement.

VII. No game shall be played between any Club member of either Association party hereto and any other Club that presents in its nine any ineligible player. *Provided* that in case the Club employing such ineligible player shall discharge him from its service, Clubs of the Associations parties hereto may thereafter play against such Club.

VIII. No Club shall pay to any of its players for one season's services a salary in excess of two thousand dollars ; nor shall any Club employing a player for any portion of the season pay said player for his services at a rate in excess of said maximum of salary, nor advance payment for such services prior to the first day of April in any year, except a sum of money in the month of March sufficient to pay for the transportation of such player from his domicile to the city where such Club is located. *Provided* that any player to whom the provisions of this Agreement applies whose services are required by any Club member of the Associations parties hereto, shall be entitled to receive for his services at least one thousand dollars.

IX. A Board of Arbitration, consisting of three duly accredited representatives from each of the Associations parties hereto, shall convene annually at a place mutually to be arranged, and shall organize by the election of a chairman, secretary and such other officers and committees as to them shall seem meet and proper. They may make, and from time to time revoke, alter and repeal all necessary rules and regulations not inconsistent with this Agreement, or with the Constitution of either Association for their meetings, procedure and the general transaction of their business. Their membership on said Board shall be determinable at the pleasure of their respective appointing Associations upon duly certified notice thereof. A quorum shall consist of at least two representatives from each Association, and all questions shall be voted upon separately by the respective delegations, and no such changes or additions shall be made unless concurred in by a majority of the delegates of each Association.

X. In addition to all matters that may be specially referred to them by both of the Associations parties hereto, the said Board shall have sole, exclusive and final jurisdiction of all disputes and complaints arising under, and all interpretations of this Agreement. They shall also, in the interests of harmony and peace, arbitrate upon and decide all differences and disputes arising between the Associations parties hereto, and between a Club member of one and a Club member of the other Association party hereto. *Provided*, that nothing in this Agreement shall be construed as giving authority to said Board to pass upon, alter, amend or modify any section or part of section of the Constitution of either Association party hereto.

We hereby certify that the said Associations parties hereto have, by a unanimous vote of the Clubs of said Associations, adopted, ratified and approved this Agreement:

N. E. YOUNG,
President of the National League of Professional B. B. Clubs.

W. C. WIKOFF,
President of the American Association of B. B. Clubs.

March 5, 1888.

ARTICLES OF QUALIFIED ADMISSION

TO THE NATIONAL AGREEMENT OF PROFESSIONAL BASE
BALL CLUBS.

The parties of the first part being the parties to the National Agreement of Professional Base Ball Clubs (viz.: the National League of Professional Base Ball Clubs and the American Association of Base Ball Clubs), and the parties of the second part being such eligible professional or semi-professional associations, each with a membership of at least six Base Ball Clubs, as shall duly authorize their Presidents to sign this agreement, and whose Presidents do sign this agreement in pursuance to said authority, do hereby agree each with the other, in consideration of the mutual advantages and protections to be derived therefrom, as follows:

I. Each Association constituting one of the parties of the second part, when it shall have signed this agreement in pursuance to authority given its President in accordance with the provisions herein, shall be, and each of them is, hereby given and afforded the following protection and qualified admission to the National Agreement of Professional Base Ball Clubs, and this in lieu of all previous contracts made by the parties to the National Agreement of Professional Base Ball Clubs with the said parties of the second part, or any of them. Provided, however, any Association whose membership shall at any time be reduced to less than four Clnbs actually engaged in a schedule of championship games, shall forfeit all rights and privileges under these articles.

II. On or after the twentieth day of October of each year, the Secretary of each Association which is a party of the second part, shall forward to the Secretary of each Association party of the first part, the names of any and all players then under contract who have signed such contracts on or after the twentieth day of October, with any of the clubs members of the said Associations, parties of the second part, and from and after the receipt of such notice, and of notice of all subsequent contracts from such Secretaries, any and all players so reported as being under contract with any of the Clubs, members of the Associations, parties of the second part, shall, unless released, be ineligible to contract with any club member of the parties of the first or second part until the 20th day of October then next ensuing; and not then if reserved under the provisions of Article X.

III. Any player who has entered into a contract with any Club member of any Association party of the second part may be suspended without pay by such Club or Association for breach of contract or breach of any of the rules of such Association, and he shall thereafter be ineligible to sign or play during the remainder of the current season with any of the Clubs of the Associations, parties to or under the protection of the National Agreement, unless such disability shall have been sooner removed by the Club or Association by which he was suspended.

IV. Any player under contract or reservation, or who shall be expelled, blacklisted, suspended or rendered ineligible by either of the parties of the first part or the Board of Arbitration, shall be ineligible to sign or play with any of the Clubs, members of the Associations parties of the second part herein, and any Club who shall knowingly play any such player, either in their Club, or shall play against any other Club who has such a player in their nine, shall be dismissed from membership by the Association of which it is a member, or said Association shall forfeit all rights under this Agreement.

V. Before any Club member of any Association, a party of the second part shall contract with a player for an ensuing season, the party of the second part of which such Club is or may be a member, shall enact laws or regulations debarring such Club from entering into such contract with such player while under arrears to him on account of his contract for the current season; also debarring such Club from suspending or otherwise attempting to disqualify a player for refusing to contract with it. Each Association party of the second part shall also enact laws providing for the expulsion of any Club member for refusal to pay arrears of salary to a player when thereto required by the Board of Directors of said Association, party of the second part, or said Association shall forfeit all rights under this Agreement.

VI. Qualified membership of any of the parties of the second part shall be forfeited for failing to expel any of its Club members that may play a game of ball, except under the Joint Playing Rules adopted by the parties of the first part, or that may play a game except with a Club member of the parties of the first part in any city; or within four miles thereof; wherein is located a Club member of the parties of the first part, without the consent of said Club.

VII. It is understood and agreed by and between the parties hereto, that any controversy between the Associations, or be-

ARTICLES OF QUALIFIED ADMISSION.

tween Clubs of different Associations parties to this Agreement, as to any matter or matters herein mentioned, or mentioned in the National Agreement, shall be determined by the Board of Arbitration without regard to any law or regulation of any party hereto, that may be in conflict therewith.

VIII. It is expressly stipulated that in any case coming before the Board of Arbitration involving the forfeiture of any rights or privileges of any Association party of the second part, or any Club member thereof, the Secretary of the said Board shall notify such Association in writing, and on demand of said party of the second part said Board shall grant it a hearing on the trial of the case, and no adverse verdict shall be rendered by said Board against such Association party of the second part, nor against any Club member thereof, unless such notice be furnished, and such hearing, if thereupon demanded, granted.

IX. Each Association, a party of the second part, shall pay to the Secretary of the Board of Arbitration:

FIRST.—As annual dues the sum of $50, on or before the first day of March in each year.

SECOND.—Also, if the right of reservation is claimed under Article X, the sum of $1,500 if said Association be composed of six clubs, or $2,000 if composed of not more than eight clubs, payable on or before the first day of May in each year.

X. The right of reservation may be claimed by any Association party of the second part by written notice to the Secretary of the Board of Arbitration on or before, and not later than the first day of March in each year, and said right of reservation will be granted under the following conditions:

FIRST.—The payment of the sum prescribed in Section 2 of Article IX, on a date not later than therein designated.

SECOND.—That the Secretary of each Association party of the second part shall on or before the 10th day of October of each year transmit to the Secretaries of both the Associations parties of the first part, a reserve list of players not exceeding fourteen in number, then under contract with each of the several Club members of the Association of which he is Secretary, and such players shall thereafter during the ensuing season, unless duly released, be ineligible to contract with any Club member of any Association party hereto, other than their respective reserving clubs.

THIRD.—That each Association entitled to the right of reservation under this Article may be represented at and participate in any discussion before the Board of Arbitration, affecting its privileges thereunder.

XI. All contracts or agreements heretofore made between the parties are hereby declared null and void.

REGULATIONS OF THE BOARD OF ARBITRATION.

I. The Officers of the Board shall be a Chairman and a Secretary, who shall also be Treasurer, who shall be elected at the regular meeting of the Board to be held in December each year. The term of each officer shall be one year, or until his successor shall have been elected and qualified, provided that any vacancy occurring by resignation or disqualification during the said term shall be filled by a majority vote of the Board, which vote may be taken by correspondence.

II. It shall be the duty of the Chairman of the Board of Arbitration to preside at all its meetings, and he shall call special meetings when he may deem it necessary, or when thereto requested by half of the members thereof. All inquiries as to the interpretation of any provision of the National Agreement, or of any agreement supplementary thereto, should be addressed to, and answered by, the Chairman of the Board.

III. The Secretary shall have the custody of all official records and papers of the Board, shall keep a record of all its meetings, and shall issue all official notices. All applications of admission to the benefits of the National Agreement should be addressed to, and answered by the Secretary of the Board of Arbitration.

IV. The regular meeting of the Board of Arbitration shall be held on the Tuesday previous to the second Wednesday in December of each year, at such place as the Chairman shall direct.

THE BOARD OF ARBITRATION, 1888.

John I. Rogers (National League), *Chairman.*
     138 South Sixth St., Philadelphia, Pa.

C. H. Byrne (American Association), *Secretary and Treasurer.*
     Fifth Av. and Fourth St., Brooklyn, N. Y.

ASSOCIATIONS IDENTIFIED WITH THE NATIONAL AGREEMENT. 107

N. E. Young (National League),
       P. O. Box 536, Washington, D. C.

Zach Phelps (American Association),
       Kendall Building, Louisville, Ky.

John B. Day (National League),
       121 Maiden Lane, N. Y. City.

Chris. Von der Ahe (American Association).
       St. Louis and Grand Av., St. Louis, Mo.

ASSOCIATIONS IDENTIFIED WITH THE NATIONAL AGREEMENT, MARCH 5, 1888.

THE NATIONAL LEAGUE OF PROFESSIONAL BASE BALL CLUBS.

N. E. Young, *Pres. and Sec.*, P. O. Box 536, Washington, D. C.

THE AMERICAN ASSOCIATION OF BASE BALL CLUBS.

Wheeler C. Wikoff, *Pres. and Sec.*, Columbus, O.

THE INTER-NATIONAL LEAGUE OF PROFESSIONAL BASE BALL CLUBS.

E. Strachan Cox, *President*, Toronto, Canada.
C. D. White, *Secretary*, Utica, N. Y.

THE WESTERN ASSOCIATION OF BASE BALL CLUBS.

S. G. Morton, *President and Secretary*, Chicago, Ill.

NEW ENGLAND LEAGUE OF PROFESSIONAL BASE BALL CLUBS.

Edwards Cheney, *President*, Lowell, Mass.
Edward F. Stevens, *Secretary*, Boston, Mass.

THE CENTRAL LEAGUE OF PROFESSIONAL BASE BALL CLUBS.

John W. Collins, *President*, Newark, N. J.
J. C. Kennedy, *Secretary*, New York City.

THE TRI-STATE LEAGUE OF BASE BALL CLUBS.

W. H. McDermith, *President*, Columbus, O.
J. B. K. Connelly, *Secretary*, Columbus, O.

THE CENTRAL INTER-STATE LEAGUE OF PROFESSIONAL BASE BALL CLUBS.

W. H. Allen, *President*, Rockford, Ill.
A. H. Spink, *Secretary*, St. Louis, Mo.

THE TEXAS LEAGUE OF BASE BALL CLUBS.

Fred. W. Turner, *President*, Austin, Tex.
W. L. Reynolds, *Secretary*, Dallas, Tex.

THE WESTERN LEAGUE OF BASE BALL CLUBS.

Wm. McClintock, *President*, Denver, Col.
A. H. Spink, *Secretary*, St. Louis, Mo.

THE SOUTHERN LEAGUE OF BASE BALL CLUBS.

J. T. Wilson, *President and Secretary*, Birmingham, Ala.

INDEX.

—TO—

RULES AND REGULATIONS.

	RULE.
The Ground...	1
The Infield...	2
The Bases..	3
The Foul Lines..	4
The Pitcher's Lines...................................	5
The Catcher's Lines...................................	6
The Captain's Lines...................................	7
The Players' Lines....................................	8
The Players' Bench....................................	9
The Batsman's Lines...................................	10
The Three Feet Lines..................................	11
The Lines Must be Marked..............................	12
The Ball..	13
Weight and Size............................(1)	13
Number Balls Furnished.....................(2)	
Furnished by Home Club.....................(2)	13
Replaced if Injured........................(4)	13
The Bat...	14

FIELD RULES.

Open Betting and Pool Selling Prohibited...............	15
No Person Allowed on Field during Game.................	16
Players not to Sit with Spectators.....................	17
Penalty for Insulting Umpire...........................	18
Penalty for not Keeping Field Clear....................	19
Restriction as to Addressing Audience..................	20
Number of Players in the Field.........................	21

THE PLAYERS AND THEIR POSITIONS.

	RULE.
Players' Positions..	22
in the Field..............................(1)	22
at the Bat................................(2)	22
Order of Batting......................(3)	22
Restriction as to Occupying Catcher's Lines...(4)	22

DEFINITIONS.

A Fair Ball...	23
An Unfair Ball..	24
A Balk...	25
A Dead Ball...	26
A Block..	27
A Fair Hit..	28
A Foul Hit...	29
A Ball Passing Outside Grounds.....................	30
A Strike...	31
A Foul Strike..	32
"Play"..	33
"Time"...	34
"Game"..	35
An Inning..	36
A Time at Bat...	37
Legal or Legally...	38

THE GAME.

Number of Innings...	39
Drawn Game..	40
Forfeited Game..	41
"No Game"..	41
Substitute, when Allowed..............................	43
Choice of Innings..	44
When Umpire Must Call "Play".....................	45
Umpire Calls Balls...	46
When Umpire May Suspend Play...................	46
" " " Terminate Game...................	46
Rain, Effect of, in Terminating Game............	46
Batsman Must Call for Ball He Wants...........	46
What Umpire Must Count and Call...............	46
When Batsman is Out...................................	47
" " Becomes Base Runner......................	48
Base Runner Must Touch Bases in Order........	49
" " When Entitled to Hold Base............	49
" " " " Take One Base...........	50
" " " Required to Return to Base...........	51

INDEX TO PLAYING RULES.   111

	RULE.
No Substitute Allowed for Base Runner	52
When Base Runner is Out	53
When Umpire Shall, without Appeal Declare Player "Out"	54
When Ball is not in Play until Returned to Pitcher	55
Block, Effect of	56
Run, when to be Scored	57
Captain only to Address Umpire	58
Coaching Restrictions	59
Umpire's Duties	60
Fines by Umpire	61
Reversing Decision	62

THE UMPIRE.

Changing Umpire	63
Duties as to Materials of Game	65
" " Ground Rules	65
" " Reversal of Decision	65
Changing Umpire during Game	65
Expulsion of Umpire	65
Umpire's Jurisdiction and Powers	65
Umpire to Give Notice of Fine	65
" " " " Forfeited Game	65
Special Penalties	65
SCORING REGULATIONS	66

CONSTITUTION AND AMENDMENTS.

Amendments of Rules	67

NATIONAL PLAYING RULES

—OF—

Professional Base Ball Clubs

AS ADOPTED JOINTLY BY THE NATIONAL LEAGUE AND AMERICAN ASSOCIATION, GOVERNING ALL CLUBS PARTIES TO THE NATIONAL AGREEMENT, 1888.

THE MATERIALS OF THE GAME.

RULE 1. The Ground must be an inclosed field, sufficient in size to enable each player to play in his position as required by these Rules.

RULE 2. The Infield must be a space of ground thirty yards square.

RULE 3. The Bases must be

(1) Four in number, and designated as First Base, Second Base, Third Base and Home Base.

(2) The Home Base must be of whitened rubber twelve inches square, so fixed in the ground as to be even with the surface, and so placed in the corner of the infield that two of its sides will form part of the boundaries of said infield.

(3) The First, Second and Third Bases must be canvas bags, fifteen inches square, painted white, and filled with some soft material, and so placed that the center of the second base shall be upon its corner of the infield, and the center of the first and third bases shall be on the lines running to and from second base and seven and one-half inches from the foul lines, providing that each base shall be entirely within the foul lines.

(4) All the Bases must be securely fastened in their positions, and so placed as to be distinctly seen by the Umpire.

RULE 4. The Foul Lines must be drawn in straight lines from the outer corner of the Home Base, along the outer edge of the First and Third Bases, to the boundaries of the Ground.

RULE 5 (SEC. 1). The Pitcher's Lines must be straight lines forming the boundaries of a space of ground, in the infield, five and one-half feet long by four feet wide, distant fifty feet from the center of Home Base, and so placed that the five and one-half feet lines would each be two feet distant from and parallel with a straight line passing through the center of the Home and Second Bases. Each corner of this space must be marked by a flat iron plate or stone, six inches square, fixed in the ground, even with the surface.

(SEC. 2.) The pitcher shall take his position facing the batsman, with both feet square on the ground, the right foot on the rear line of the "box," his left foot in front of the right, and to the left of an imaginary line from his right foot to the center of the home base. He shall not raise his right foot, unless in the act of delivering the ball, nor make more than one step in such delivery. He shall hold the ball, before the delivery, fairly in front of his body, and in sight of the Umpire. In the case of a left-handed pitcher the above words "left" and "right" are to be reversed. When the pitcher feigns to throw the ball to a base he must resume the above position and pause momentarily before delivering the ball to the bat.

RULE 6. The Catcher's Lines must be drawn from the outer corner of the Home Base, in continuation of the Foul Lines, straight to the limits of the Ground back of Home Base.

RULE 7. The Captain's or Coacher's Lines must be a line fifteen feet from and parallel with the Foul Lines, said lines commencing at a line parallel with and seventy-five feet distant from the catcher's line, and running thence to the limits of the grounds. And should the said Captain or Coacher wilfully fail to remain in said bounds, he shall be fined by the Umpire five dollars for each such offence, except upon an appeal by the Captain from the Umpire's decision upon a misinterpretation of the rules.

RULE 8. The Player's Lines must be drawn from the Catcher's Lines to the limits of the Ground, fifty feet distant from and parallel with, the foul lines.

RULE 9. The Players' Benches must be furnished by the home club, and placed upon a portion of the ground outside the Players' Lines. They must be twelve feet in length, and must be immovably fastened to the ground. At the end of each bench must be immovably fixed a bat-rack, with fixtures for holding twenty bats; one such rack must be designated for the exclusive use of the Visiting Club, and the other for the exclusive use of the Home Club.

RULE 10. The Batsman's Lines must be straight lines forming the boundaries of a space on the right, and of a similar space on the left of the Home Base, six feet long by four feet wide, extending three feet in front of and three feet behind the center of the Home Base, and with its nearest line distant six inches from the Home Base.

RULE 11. The Three Feet Lines must be drawn as follows: From a point on the Foul Line from Home Base to First Base, and equally distant from such bases, shall be drawn a line on Foul Ground, at a right angle to said Foul Line, and to a point three feet distant from it; thence running parallel with said Foul Line, to a point three feet distant from the First Base; thence in a straight line to the Foul Line, and thence upon the Foul Line to point of beginning.

RULE 12. The lines designated in Rules 4, 5, 6, 7, 8, 10 and 11 must be marked with chalk or other suitable material, so as to be distinctly seen by the Umpire. They must all be so marked their entire length, except the Captain's and Players' Lines, which must be so marked for a distance of at least thirty-five yards from the Catcher's Lines.

RULE 13. The Ball.*

(SECTION 1.) Must not weigh less than five nor more than five and one-quarter ounces avoirdupois, and measure not less than nine nor more than nine and one-quarter inches in circumference. The Spalding League Ball, or the Reach American Association Ball must be used in all games played under these rules.

(SEC. 2.) For each championship game two balls shall be furnished by the Home Club to the Umpire for use. When the ball in play is batted over the fence or stands, on to foul ground out of sight of the players, the other ball shall be immediately put into play by the Umpire. As often as one of the two in use shall be lost, a new one must be substituted, so that the Umpire may at all times, after the game begins, have two for use. The moment the Umpire delivers the alternate ball to the catcher or pitcher it comes into play, and shall not be exchanged until it, in turn, passes out of sight on to foul ground.

(SEC. 3) In all games the ball or balls played with shall be furnished by the Home Club, and the last ball in play becomes

---

*THE SPALDING LEAGUE BALL has been the official ball of the National League for the past ten years, and has again been adopted for 1888. It is in general use by all the leading professional, college and amateur clubs throughout the country, and stands without a rival as the best ball made.

The Spalding Ball has been officially adopted and used exclusively by the following associations:

The National League; Western Association International League; Northwestern League; Central League; Western League; New England League; N. Y. Inter-state League; Canadian League; Inter-state League; California League; Central Inter-state League; American College Association; N. W. College Association, and nearly all the minor State and City leagues throughout the United States and Canada. *Beware of counterfeits;* none genuine without the Spalding Trade Mark on each box and ball.

the property of the winning club. Each ball to be used in championship games shall be examined, measured and weighed by the Secretary of the Association, inclosed in a paper box and sealed with the seal of the Secretary, which seal shall not be broken except by the umpire in the presence of the captains of the two contesting nines after play has been called.

(Sec. 4.) Should the ball become out of shape, or cut or ripped so as to expose the yarn, or in any way so injured as to be—in the opinion of the Umpire—unfit for fair use, the Umpire, on being appealed to by either captain, shall at once put the alternate ball into play and call for a new one.

Rule 14. The Bat.

(1) Must be made wholly of wood, except that the handle may be wound with twine, or a granulated substance applied, not to exceed eighteen inches from the end.

(2) It must be round except that a portion of the surface may be flat on one side, must not exceed two and one-half inches in diameter in the thickest part, and must not exceed forty-two inches in length.

FIELD RULES.

Rule 15. No Club shall allow open betting or pool selling upon its grounds, nor in any building owned or occupied by it.

Rule 16. No person shall be allowed upon any part of the field during the progress of the game, in addition to the players in uniform, the manager on each side and the umpire; except such officers of the law as may be present in uniform, and such officials of the Home Club as may be necessary to preserve the peace.

Rule 17. Players in uniform shall not be permitted to seat themselves among the spectators.

Rule 18. The Umpire is the sole judge of play, and is entitled to the respect of the spectators, and any person offering any insult or indignity to him, must be promptly ejected from the grounds.

Rule 19. Every club shall furnish sufficient police force upon its own grounds to preserve order, and in the event of a crowd entering the field during the progress of a game, and interfering with the play in any manner, the Visiting Club may refuse to play further until the field be cleared. If the ground be not cleared within fifteen minutes thereafter, the Visiting Club may claim, and shall be entitled to, the game by a score of nine runs to none (no matter what number of innings have been played).

Rule 20. No Umpire, Manager, Captain or Player shall address the audience during the progress of a game, except in case of necessary explanation.

THE PLAYERS AND THEIR POSITIONS.

RULE 21. The Players of each club in a match game shall be nine in number, one of whom shall act as Captain. Every Club shall be required to adopt uniforms for its players, and in no case shall less than nine men be allowed to play on each side. Each player shall be required to present himself upon the field during said game in a neat and cleanly condition, but no player shall attach anything to the sole or heel of his shoes other than the ordinary base ball shoe plate.

RULE 22. The Players' position shall be

SECTION 1. When in the field (designated "Fielders" in these Rules) such as may be assigned them by their Captain, except that the Pitcher must take his position within the Pitcher's Lines, as defined in Rule 5.

SEC. 2. When their side goes to the bat they must immediately seat themselves upon the players' bench and remain there until the side is put out, except when batsman or base runner. All bats not in use must be kept in the bat racks, and the two players next succeeding the batsman, in the order in which they are named on the score, must be ready with bat in hand to promptly take position as batsman; provided, that the Captain and one assistant only may occupy the space between the players' lines and the Captain's lines to coach base runners.

(SEC. 3.) The Batsmen must take their positions within the Batsmen's Lines, as defined in Rule 10, in the order in which they are named on *the score*, which must contain the batting order of both nines, and be submitted to and approved by the Umpire before the game, and must be followed, except in case of disability of a player, in which case the substitute must take the place of the disabled player in the batting order. "After the first inning the first striker in each inning shall be the batsman whose name follows that of the last man who has completed his turn—time—at bat in the preceding inning."

SEC. 4. No player of the side at bat, except when Batsman, shall occupy any portion of the space within the Catcher's Lines, as defined in Rule 6.

DEFINITIONS.

RULE 23. A Fair Ball is a ball delivered by the Pitcher while standing wholly within the lines of his position, and facing the batsman, the ball, so delivered to pass over the home base, not lower than the batsman's knee, nor higher than his shoulder.

RULE 24. An Unfair Ball is a ball delivered by the Pitcher, as in Rule 23, except that the ball does not pass over the Home Base, or does pass over the Home Base above the batsman's shoulder, or below the knee.

RULE 25. A Balk is

(SEC. 1.) Any motion made by the Pitcher to deliver the ball to the bat without delivering it, and shall be held to include any and every accustomed motion with the hands, arms or feet, or position of the body assumed by the Pitcher in his delivery of the ball, and any motion calculated to deceive a base runner, except the ball be accidentally dropped.

(SEC. 2.) If the ball be held by the pitcher so long as to delay the game unnecessarily; or

(SEC. 3.) Any motion to deliver the ball, or the delivering the ball to the bat by the Pitcher when any part of his person is upon ground outside of the lines of his position, including all preliminary motions with the hands, arms and feet.

RULE 26. A Dead Ball is a ball delivered to the bat by the Pitcher that touches the Batsman's bat without being struck at, or any part of the Batsman's person or clothing while standing in his position without being struck at; or any part of the Umpire's person or clothing without first passing the Catcher.

RULE 27. A Block is a batted or thrown ball that is stopped or handled by any person not engaged in the game.

RULE 28. A Fair Hit is a ball batted by the Batsman, standing in his position, that first touches the ground, the First Base, the Third Base, the part of the person of a player, or any other object that is in front of or on either of the Foul Lines, or (exception) batted directly to the ground by the Batsman, standing in his position, that (whether it first touches Foul or Fair Ground) bounds or rolls within the Foul Lines, between Home and First, or Home and Third Bases, without first touching the person of a player.

RULE 29. A Foul Hit is a ball batted by the Batsman, standing in his position, that first touches the ground, the part of the person of a player, or any other object that is behind either of the Foul Lines, or that strikes the person of such Batsman, while standing in his position, or (exception) batted directly to the ground by the Batsman, standing in his position, that (whether it first touches Foul or Fair Ground) bounds or rolls outside the Foul Lines, between Home and First or Home and Third Bases, without first touching the person of a player.

RULE 30. When a batted ball passes outside the grounds, the Umpire shall decide it fair should it disappear within, or foul should it disappear outside of the range of the Foul Lines, and Rules 28 and 29 are to be construed accordingly.

RULE 31. A Strike is

(1.) A ball struck at by the Batsman without its touching his bat; or

(2.) A Fair Ball, legally delivered by the Pitcher, but not struck at by the Batsman.

(3.) Any obvious attempt to make a foul hit.

RULE 32. A Foul Strike is a ball batted by the Batsman when any part of his person is upon ground outside the lines of the batsman's position.

RULE 33. Play is the order of the Umpire to begin the game, or to resume play after its suspension.

RULE 34. Time is the order of the Umpire to suspend play. Such suspension must not extend beyond the day of the game.

RULE 35. Game is the announcement by the Umpire that the game is terminated.

RULE 36. An Innings is the term at bat of the nine players representing a Club in a game, and is completed when three of such players have been put out as provided in these Rules.

RULE 37. A Time at Bat is the term at bat of a Batsman. It begins when he takes his position, and continues until he is put out or becomes a base runner; except when, because of being hit by a pitched ball, or in case of an illegal delivery by the Pitcher, as in Rule 48.

RULE 38. Legal or Legally signifies as required by these Rules.

THE GAME.

RULE 39. A Game shall consist of nine innings to each contesting nine, except that,

(1.) If the side first at bat scores less runs in nine innings than the other side has scored in eight innings, the game shall then terminate.

(2.) If the side last at bat in the ninth inning scores the winning run before the third man is out, the game shall then terminate.

(3.) If the score be a tie at the end of nine innings to each side, play shall only be continued until the side first at bat shall have scored one or more runs than the other side, in an equal number of innings, or until the other side shall score one more run than the side first at bat.

(4.) If the Umpire calls "Game" on account of darkness or rain at any time after five innings have been completed by both sides, the score shall be that of the last equal innings played, unless the side second at bat shall have scored one or more runs than the side first at bat, in which case the score of the game shall be the total number of runs made.

RULE 40. A Drawn Game shall be declared by the Umpire

when he terminates a game on account of darkness or rain, after five equal innings have been played, if the score at the time is equal on the last even innings played; but (exception) if the side that went second to bat is then at the bat, and has scored the same number of runs as the other side, the Umpire shall declare the game drawn, without regard to the score of the last equal innings.

RULE 41. A Forfeited Game shall be declared by the Umpire n favor of the Club not in fault, in the following cases :

(1.) If the nine of a club fail to appear upon the field, or being upon the field, fail to begin the game within five minutes after the Umpire has called "Play," at the hour appointed for the beginning of the game, unless such delay in appearing or in commencing the game, be unavoidable.

(2.) If, after the game has begun, one side refuses or fails to continue playing, unless such game has been suspended or terminated by the Umpire.

(3.) If, after play has been suspended by the Umpire, one side fails to resume playing within five minutes after the Umpire has called "Play."

(4.) If, in the opinion of the Umpire, any one of these Rules is willfully violated.

RULE 42. "No Game" shall be declared by the Umpire if he shall terminate play on account of rain or darkness, before five innings on each side are completed.

RULE 43. A substitute shall not be allowed to take the place of any player in a game, unless such player be disabled in the game then being played, by reason of illness or injury of the nature or extent of which the Umpire shall be sole judge.

RULE 44. The choice of innings shall be,

(1.) Given to the Captain of the Home Club, who shall also be the sole judge of the fitness of the ground for beginning a game after rain, and no game shall be begun later than two hours before sunset.

(2.) In every championship game each team shall be required to have present on the field, in uniform, at least one or more players, and no player except he be so in uniform shall be substituted for any sick or injured player.

RULE 45. The Umpire must call "Play," at the hour appointed for beginning a game. The game must begin when the Umpire calls "Play." When he calls "Time," play shall be suspended until he calls "Play" again, and during the interim no player shall be put out, base be run, or run be scored. The Umpire shall suspend play only for an accident to himself or a player (but in case of accident to a Fielder, Time shall not be called until the ball be returned to, and held by the Pitcher, standing in his position), or in case rain falls so heavily that the spectators are compelled, by the severity of the storm, to seek shelter, in which case he shall note the time of suspension, and should such rain continue to fall thirty minutes thereafter, he shall terminate the game; or to enforce order in case of annoyance from spectators. The Umpire shall also declare every "Dead Ball," "Block," "Foul Hit," "Foul Strike," and "Balk."

RULE 46. The Umpire shall count and call every "unfair ball" delivered by the Pitcher, and every "dead ball," if also an unfair ball, as a "ball," and he shall also count and call every "strike." Neither a "ball" nor a "strike" shall be counted or called until the ball has passed the home base.

RULE 47. The batsman is out:

(1). If he fails to take his position at the bat in his order of batting, unless the error be discovered and the proper Batsman takes his position before a fair hit has been made, and in such case the balls and strikes called will be counted in the time at bat of the proper Batsman.

(2.) If he fails to take his position within one minute after the Umpire has called for the Batsman.

(3.) If he makes a Foul Hit, and the ball be momentarily held by a Fielder before touching the ground, provided it be not caught in a Fielder's hat or cap, or touch some object other than a Fielder before being caught.

(4.) If he makes a Foul Strike.

(5.) If he plainly attempts to hinder the Catcher from fielding the ball, evidently without effort to make a fair hit.

(6). If. while the First Base be occupied by a base runner, three strikes be called on him by the Umpire, except when two hands are already out.

(7.) If, while making the third strike the ball hits his person or clothing.

(8.) If, after two strikes have been called, the Batsman obviously attempts to make a foul hit as in Section 3, Rule 31.

RULE 48. The Batsman becomes a Base Runner :

(1.) Instantly after he makes a Fair Hit.

(2.) Instantly after five Balls have been called by the Umpire.

(3.) Instantly after three Strikes have been declared by the Umpire.

(4.) If, while he be a Batsman, his person or clothing be hit by a ball from the pitcher, unless—in the opinion of the Umpire—he intentionally permits himself to be so hit.

(5.) Instantly after an illegal delivery of a ball by the pitcher.

RULE 49. The Base Runner must touch each Base in regular order, viz.: First, Second, Third and Home Bases; and when obliged to return, must retouch the base or bases in reverse order. He shall only be considered as holding a base after touching it, and shall then be entitled to hold such base until he has legally touched the next base in order, or has been legally forced to vacate it for a succeeding Base Runner.

RULE 50. The Base Runner shall be entitled, without being put out, to take one Base in the following cases:

(1.) If, while he was Batsman, the Umpire called five Balls.

(2.) If the Umpire awards a succeeding Batsman a base on five balls, or for being hit with a pitched ball, or in case of an illegal delivery—as in Rule 48—and the Base Runner is thereby forced to vacate the base held by him.

(3.) If the Umpire calls a "balk."

(4.) If a ball delivered by the Pitcher pass the Catcher and touch the Umpire or any fence or building within ninety feet of the Home Base.

(5.) If he be prevented from making a base by the obstruction of an adversary.

(6.) If the Fielder stop or catch a batted ball with his hat or any part of his dress.

RULE 51. The Base Runner shall return to his Base, and shall be entitled to so return without being put out.

(1.) If the Umpire declares a Foul Hit, and the ball be not legally caught by a Fielder.

(2.) If the Umpire declares a Foul Strike.

(3.) If the Umpire declares a Dead Ball, unless it be also the fifth Unfair Ball, and he be thereby forced to take the next base, as provided in Rule 50. (See clause 2.)

RULE 52. The Base Runner shall not have a substitute run for him.

RULE 53, The Base Runner is out:

(1.) If, after three Strikes have been declared against him while Batsman, and the Catcher fail to catch the third strike ball, he plainly attempts to hinder the Catcher from fielding the ball.

(2.) If, having made a Fair Hit while Batsman, such fair hit ball be momentarily held by a Fielder, before touching the ground or any object other than a Fielder: *Provided*, It be not caught in a Fielder's hat or cap.

(3.) If, when the Umpire has declared three strikes on him, while batsman, the third strike ball be momentarily held by a

Fielder before touching the ground. *Provided*, it be not caught in a Fielder's hat or cap, or touch some object other than a Fielder before being caught.

(4.) If, after three Strikes or a Fair Hit, he be touched with the ball in the hand of a Fielder before such Base Runner touches First Base.

(5.) If, after three Strikes or a Fair Hit, the ball be securely held by a Fielder, while touching First Base with any part of his person, before such Base Runner touches First Base.

(6.) If, in running the last half of the distance from Home Base to First Base, he runs outside the Three Feet Lines, as defined in Rule 11; except that he must do so if necessary to avoid a Fielder attempting to field a batted ball, and in such case shall not be declared out.

(7.) If, in running from First to Second Base, from Second to Third Base, or from Third to Home Base, he runs more than three feet from a direct line between such bases to avoid being touched by the ball in the hands of a Fielder; but in case a Fielder be occupying the Base Runner's proper path, attempting to field a batted ball, then the Base Runner shall run out of the path and behind said Fielder, and shall not be declared out for so doing.

(8.) If he falls to avoid a Fielder attempting to field a batted ball, in the manner prescribed in clauses 6 and 7 of this Rule; or if he, in any way, obstructs a Fielder attempting to field a batted ball, or intentionally interferes with a thrown ball: *Provided*, That if two or more Fielders attempt to field a batted ball, and the Base Runner comes in contact with one or more of them, the Umpire shall determine which Fielder is entitled to the benefit of this Rule, and shall not decide the Base Runner out for coming in contact with any other Fielder.

(9.) If, at any time while the ball is in play, he be touched by the ball in the hand of a Fielder, unless some part of his person is touching a base he is entitled to occupy; *Provided*, the ball be held by the Fielder after touching him; but (exception as to First Base), in running to First Base, he may overrun said base without being put out for being off said base, after first touching it, provided he returns at once and retouches the base, after which he may be put out as at any other base. If, in over-running First Base, he also attempts to run to Second Base, or, after passing the base he turns to his left from the foul line, he shall forfeit such exemption from being put out.

(10.) If, when a Fair or Foul Hit ball is legally caught by a Fielder, such ball is legally held by a Fielder on the base occupied by the Base Runner when such ball was struck (or the

Base Runner be touched with the ball in the hands of a Fielder), before he retouches said base after such Fair or Foul Hit ball was so caught. *Provided*, That the Base Runner shall aot be out in such case, if, after the ball was legally caught as above, it be delivered to the bat by the Pitcher before the Fielder holds it on said base, or touches the Base Runner with it; but if the Base Runner in attempting to reach a base, detaches it before being touched or forced out he shall be declared safe.

(11.) If, when a Batsman becomes a Base Ruuner (except as provided in Rule 50), the First Base, or the First and Second Bases, or the First, Second and Third Bases, be occupied, any Base Runner so occupying a base shall cease to be entitled to hold it, until any following Base Runner is put out and may be put out at the next base or by being touched by the ball in the hands of a Fielder in the same manner as in running to First Base, at any time before any following Base Runner is put out.

(12.) If a fair hit ball strike him *before touching a fielder* he shall be declared out, and in such case no base shall be run unless forced by the Batsman becoming a Base Runner, and no run be scored.

(13.) If when running to a base or forced to return to a base, he fail to touch the intervening base or bases, if any, in the order prescribed in Rule 49, he may be put out at the base he fails to touch, or by being touched by the ball in the hand of a Fielder, in the same manner as in running to First Base.

(14.) If, when the Umpire calls "Play," after any suspension of a game, he fails to return to and touch the base he occupied when "Time" was called before touching the next base.

RULE 54. The Umpire shall declare the Batsman or Base Runner out, without waiting for an appeal for such decision, in all cases where such player is put out in accordance with these rules, except as provided in Rule 53, clauses 10 and 14.

RULE 55. In case of a Foul Strike, Foul Hit ball not legally caught flying, Dead Ball, or Base Runner put out for being struck by a fair-hit ball, the ball shall not be considered in play until it is held by the Pitcher standing in his position.

RULE 56. Whenever a Block occurs, the Umpire shall declare it, and Base Runners may run the bases, without being put out, until after the ball has been returned to and held by the Pitcher standing in his position.

RULE 57. One Run shall be scored every time a Base Runner, after having legally touched the first three bases, shall touch the Home Base before three men are put out. If the third man is forced out, or is put out before reaching First Base, a run shall not be scored.

RULE 58. The Captain only may address the Umpire, and then only, upon a question of interpretation of the rules. Any violation of this rule shall subject the offender to a fine of five dollars by the Umpire.

RULE 59. The Captains and Coachers are restricted in coaching to the Base Runner only, and are not allowed to address any remarks except to the Base Runner, and then only in words of necessary direction; and no player shall use language which will, in any manner, refer to or reflect upon a player of the opposing club, or the audience. To enforce the above the Captain of the opposite side may call the attention of the Umpire to the offence and upon a repetition of the same the club shall be debarred from further coaching during the game.

THE UMPIRE'S DUTIES.

RULE 60. The Umpire's duties shall be as follows:

(1.) The Umpire is the sole and absolute judge of play. In no instance shall any person be allowed to question the correctness of any decision made by him except the Captains of the contending nines, and no other player shall at such time leave his position in the field, his place at the bat, on the bases or players' bench, to approach or address the Umpire in word or act upon such disputed decision, unless requested to do so by the Umpire. Every player violating this provision shall be fined by said Umpire ten dollars for each offence. Neither shall any Manager or other officers of either club except the Captains as before mentioned—be permitted to go upon the field or address the Umpire in regard to such disputed decision under a penalty of a forfeiture of the game to the opposing club. The Umpire shall in no case appeal to any spectator for information in regard to any such case, but may ask for information, if he so desires, from one or more of the players.

(2.) Before the commencement of a Match Game, the Umpire shall see that the rules governing all the materials of the game are strictly observed. He shall ask the Captain of the Home Club whether there are any special ground rules to be enforced, and if there are, he shall see that they are duly enforced, provided they do not conflict with any of these Rules. He shall also ascertain whether the fence in the rear of the Catcher's position is distant ninety feet from the Home Base.

(3.) In case the Umpire imposes a fine on a player, or declares a game forfeited, he shall transmit a written notice thereof to the President of the Association within twenty-four hours thereafter, under the penalty of having said fine taken from his own salary.

RULE 61. The umpire's jurisdiction and powers in addition to those specified in the constitution and the preceding rules are:

(1,) He must keep the contesting nines playing constantly from the commencement of the game to its termination, allowing such delays only as are rendered unavoidable by accident, injury or rain. He must, until the completion of the game, require the players of each side to promptly take their positions in the field as soon as the third hand is put out, and must require the first striker of the opposite side to be in his position at the bat as soon as the fielders are in their places.

(2) The players of the side "at bat" must occupy the portion of the field allotted them, but must speedily vacate any portion thereof that may be in the way of the ball, or of any Fielder attempting to catch or field it. The triangular space behind the Home Base is reserved for the exclusive use of the Umpire, Catcher and Batsman, and the Umpire must prohibit any player of the side "at bat" from crossing the same at any time while the ball is in the hands of, or passing between, the Pitcher and Catcher, while standing in their positions.

(3) The Umpire is master of the Field from the commencement to the termination of the game, and must compel the players to observe the provisions of all the Playing Rules, and he is hereby invested with authority to order any player to do or omit to do any act, as he may deem it necessary to give force and effect to any and all of such provisions, and powers to inflict upon any player disobeying any such order a fine of not less than five nor more than twenty-five dollars for each offence, and to impose a similar fine upon any player who shall use abusive, threatening or improper language to the Umpire.

(4) The Umpire shall at once notify the Captain of the offending player's side of the infliction of any fine herein provided for.

RULE 62. A fair batted ball that goes over the fence at a less distance than two hundred and ten feet from Home Base shall entitle the Batsman to two bases and a distinctive line shall be marked on the fence at this point. The Umpire shall not reverse his decision on any point of play upon the testimony of any player engaged in the game, or upon the testimony of any bystander.

RULE 63. The Umpire shall not be changed during the progress of a game, except for reason of illness or injury.

RULE 64. For the special benefit of the patrons of the game, and because the offences specified are under his immediate jurisdiction, and not subject to appeal by players, the attention of the Umpire is particularly directed to possible violations of the purpose and spirit of the Rules of the following character :

(1.) Laziness or loafing of players in taking their places in the field, or those allotted them by the Rules when their side is at the bat, and especially any failure to keep the bats in the racks provided for them ; to be ready (two men) to take position as Batsmen, and to remain upon the Players' Bench, except when otherwise required by the Rules.

(2.) Any attempt by players of the side at bat, by calling to a Fielder, other than the one designated by his Captain, to field a ball, or by any other equally disreputable means seeking to disconcert a Fielder.

(3.) Indecent or improper language addressed by a player to the audience, the Umpire, or any player. In any of these cases the Umpire must promptly fine the offending player.

(4.) The Rules make a marked distinction between hindrance of an adversary in fielding a batted or thrown ball. This has been done to rid the game of the childish excuses and claims formerly made by a Fielder failing to hold a ball to put out a Base Runner. But there may be cases of a Base Runner so flagrantly violating the spirit of the Rules and of the Game in obstructing a Fielder from fielding a thrown ball that it would become the duty of the Umpire, not only to declare the Base Runner "out" (and to compel any succeeding Base Runners to hold their bases), but also to impose a heavy fine upon him. For example: If the Base Runner plainly strike at the ball while passing him, to prevent its being caught by a Fielder; if he hold a fielder's arms so as to disable him from catching the ball, or if he run against or knock the Fielder down for the same purpose.

(5.) In the case of a "Block," if the person not engaged in the game should retain possession of the ball, or throw or kick it beyond the reach of the Fielders, the Umpire should call "Time" and require each base runner to stop at the last base touched by him until the ball be returned to the pitcher standing in his position.

(6.) The Umpire shall call "Play" at the exact time advertised for beginning a game, and any player not then ready to take the position allotted him, must be promptly fined by the Umpire.

(7.) The Umpire is only allowed, by the Rules, to call "Time" in case of an accident to himself or a player, or in case of rain, as defined by the Rules. The practice of players suspending the game to discuss or contest a decision with the Umpire, is a gross violation of the Rules, and the Umpire must promptly fine any player who interrupts the game in this manner.

SCORING.

RULE 65. In Order to Promote Uniformity in Scoring Championship Games, the following instructions, suggestions and definitions are made for the benefit of scorers, and they are required to make all scores in accordance therewith.

BATTING.

(1.) The first item in the tabulated score, after the player's name and position, shall be the number of times he has been at bat during the game. At any time or times where the player has been sent to base by being hit by a pitched ball by the pitcher's illegal delivery, or by a base on balls shall not be included in this column.

(2.) In the second column should be set down the runs made by each player.

(3.) In the third column should be placed the first base hits made by each player. A base hit should be scored in the following cases:

When the ball from the bat strike the ground between the foul lines, and out of reach of the fielders.

When a hit ball is partially or wholly stopped by a fielder in motion, but such player cannot recover himself in time to handle the ball before the striker reaches First Base.

When the ball is hit so sharply to an infielder that he cannot handle it in time to put out a man. In case of doubt over this class of hits, score a base hit and exempt the fielder from the charge of an error,

When a ball is hit so slowly toward a fielder that he cannot handle it in time to put out a man.

That in all cases where a base runner is retired by being hit by a batted ball, the batsman should be credited with a base hit.

That when a player reaches first base through an error of judgment such as two fielders allowing the ball to drop between them, the batter shall not be credited with a base hit, nor the fielder charged with an error, but it shall be scored as an unaccepted chance, and the batter shall be charged with a time at the bat.

BASE RUNNING.

(4.) In the fourth column shall be scored bases stolen, and shall be governed as follows:

Any attempt to steal a base must go to the credit of the base runner, whether the ball is thrown wild or muffed by the fielder, but any manifest error is to be charged to the fielder, making the same. If the base runner advances another base he shall not be credited with a stolen base, and the fielder allowing the advancement is also to be charged with an error. If a base runner makes a start and a battery error is made, the runner secures the credit of a stolen base, and the battery error is scored against the player making it. Should a base runner overrun a base and then be put out, he should receive the credit for the stolen base.

FIELDING.

(5.) The number of opponents put out by each player shall be set down in the fifth column. Where a striker is given out by the Umpire for a foul strike, or because he struck out of his turn, the put-out shall be scored to the Catcher.

(6.) The number of times the player assists shall be set down in the sixth column. An assist should be given to each player who handles the ball in assisting a run out or other play of the kind.

An assist should be given to a player who makes a play in time to put a runner out, even if the player who should complete the play fails, through no fault of the player assisting.

And generally an assist should be given to each player who handles the ball from the time it leaves the bat until it reaches the player who makes the put out, or in case of a thrown ball, to each player who throws or handles it cleanly and in such a way that a put-out results, or would result if no error were made by the receiver.

An assist shall be given the Pitcher when the Batsman fails to hit the ball on the third strike, and the same shall also be entered in the summary under the head of "struck out."

EARNED RUNS.

(7.) An earned run shall be scored every time the player reaches the home base unaided by errors before chances have been offered to retire the side, but bases on balls though summarized as errors, shall be credited as factors in earned runs.

(8.) An error shall be given in the seventh column for each misplay which allows the striker or base runner to make one or more bases when perfect play would have insured his being put out, except that "wild pitches," "bases on the batsman being struck by a pitched ball," or case of illegal pitched ball, balks and passed balls, shall not be included in said column. In scoring errors off batted balls see Section 3 of this Rule.

RULE 66. The Summary shall contain:

(1.) The number of earned runs made by each side.

(2.) The number of two-base hits made by each player.

(3.) The number of three-base hits made by each player.

(4.) The number of home runs made by each player.

(5.) The number of double and triple plays made by each side, with the names of the players assisting in the same.

(6.) The number of men given bases on called balls, by each Pitcher.

(7.) The number of men given bases from being hit by pitched balls.
(8.) The number of men struck out.
(9.) The number of passed balls by each Catcher.
(10.) The number of wild pitches by each Pitcher.
(11.) The time of game.
(12.) The name of the Umpire.

AMENDMENTS.

RULE 67. No Amendment or change of any of these National Playing Rules shall be made, except by a joint committee on rules, consisting of three members from the National League and three members from the American Association. Such committee to be appointed at the annual meetings of each of said bodies to serve one year from the twentieth day of December of each year. Such committee shall have full power to act, provided that such amendments shall be made only by an affirmative vote of the majority of each delegation.

NATIONAL LEAGUE SCHEDULE OF CHAMPIONSHIP GAMES FOR 1888.

CLUBS.	At Boston.	At New York.	At Philadelp'a.	At Washingt'n.	At Pittsburg.	At Detroit.	At Ind'napolis.	At Chicago.
Boston.......	....	April 30 May 1 " 2 " 3 July 23 " 24 " 25 Aug. 27 " 28 " 29	April 20 " 21 " 23 " 24 June 29 " 30 July 2 Aug. 20 " 21 " 22	April 25 " 26 " 27 " 28 July 19 " 20 " 21 Aug. 23 " 24 " 25	May 10 " 11 " 12 " 14 July 11 " 12 " 13 Sept. 20 " 21 " 22	May 5 " 7 " 8 " 9 July 14 " 16 " 17 Sept. 15 " 17 " 18	May 19 " 21 " 22 " 23 July 4 " 4 " 5 Sept. 11 " 12 " 13	May 15 " 16 " 17 " 18 July 7 " 9 " 10 Sept. 7 " 8 " 10
New York...	June 19 " 20 " 21 " 22 Aug. 2 " 3 " 4 " 30 " 31 Sept. 1	....	June 23 " 25 " 26 " 27 July 19 " 20 " 21 Aug. 23 " 24 " 25	April 20 " 21 " 23 " 24 Aug. 20 " 21 " 22 Sept. 24 " 25 " 26	May 15 " 16 " 17 " 18 July 7 " 9 " 10 Sept. 15 " 17 " 18	May 19 " 21 " 22 " 23 July 4 " 4 " 5 Sept. 20 " 21 " 22	May 5 " 7 " 8 " 9 July 11 " 12 " 13 Sept. 7 " 8 " 10	May 10 " 11 " 12 " 14 July 14 " 16 " 17 Sept. 11 " 12 " 13
Philadelphia.	May 25 " 26 " 28 " 29 July 30 " 31 Aug. 1 Sept. 24 " 25 " 26	April 25 " 26 " 27 " 28 July 26 " 27 " 28 Sept. 3 " 4 " 5	....	June 18 " 19 " 20 " 21 Aug. 2 " 3 " 4 " 27 " 28 " 29	May 5 " 7 " 8 " 9 July 14 " 16 " 17 Sept. 7 " 8 " 10	May 10 " 11 " 12 " 14 July 11 " 12 " 13 Sept. 11 " 12 " 13	May 15 " 16 " 17 " 18 July 7 " 9 " 10 Sept. 20 " 21 " 22	May 19 " 21 " 22 " 23 July 4 " 4 " 5 Sept. 15 " 17 " 18
Washington......	June 23 " 25 " 26 " 27 July 26 " 27 " 28 Sept. 3 " 4 " 5	May 25 " 26 " 28 " 29 June 29 " 30 July 2 Aug. 30 " 31 Sept. 1	April 30 May 1 " 2 " 3 July 23 " 24 " 25 Aug. 30 " 31 Sept. 1	....	May 19 " 21 " 22 " 23 July 4 " 4 " 5 Sept. 11 " 12 " 13	May 15 " 16 " 17 " 18 July 7 " 9 " 10 Sept. 7 " 8 " 10	May 10 " 11 " 12 " 14 July 14 " 16 " 17 Sept. 15 " 17 " 18	May 5 " 7 " 8 " 9 July 11 " 12 " 13 Sept. 20 " 21 " 22

City									
Pittsburg	June 2,4,5,6,7 Aug. 8,11,12,13 Oct. 3,4,5	May 30,31 June 1,9,10,11 Oct. 6,8,9	June 8,9,11,12 Aug. 16,17,18 Sept. 28,29 Oct. 1	June 13,14,15,16 Aug. 13,14,15 Oct. 3,4,5		May 1,2,3,4,23,24,25 July 2,3,4 Aug.		June 25,26,27,28,19,20,21 July Sept. 3,4,5	June 20,21,22,23,30,31 July 1,27,28,29 Aug.
Detroit	June 8,9,11,12,13,14 Aug. 15 Oct. 3,4,5	June 13,14,15,16,17,18 Sept. 28,29 Oct. 1	May 30,31 June 1,9,10,11 Oct. 6,8,9	June 2,4,5,6,7,8,11,12,13 Aug.	April 20,21,23,24,30,31 Aug. Sept. 1,24,25,26			April 26,27,28,30 June 29,30 July Aug. 20,21,22	May 24,25,26,28,26,27,28 July Sept. 3,4,5
Indianapolis	May 30,31 June 1,9,10 Oct. 6,8,9	June 2,4,5,6,7,8,11,12,13 Aug.	June 13,14,15,16,13,14,15 Oct. 3,4,5	June 8,9,11,12,16,17,18 Sept. 28,29 Oct. 1	May 24,25,26,28,26,27,28 July Aug. 23,24,25	June 20,21,22,23,30,31 July 1,27,28,29 Aug.			May 1,2,3,4,2,3 Aug. Sept. 24,26
Chicago	June 14,15,16,18,16,17,18 Sept. 28,29 Oct. 1	June 8,9,11,12,13,14,15 Oct. 3,4,5	June 2,4,5,6,7,8,11,12,13 Aug.	May 30,31 June 1,9,10,11 Oct. 6,8,9	April 26,27,28,30 June 29,30 July Aug. 20,21,22	June 25,26,27,28,19,20,21 July Aug. 23,24,25	April 20,21,23,24,30,31 July Aug. 30,31 Sept. 1		

AMERICAN ASSOCIATION SCHEDULE OF CHAMPIONSHIP GAMES FOR 1888.

CLUBS.	At Brooklyn.	At Philadelp'a.	At Baltimore.	At Cleveland.	At Cincinnati.	At Louisville.	At St. Louis.	At Kansas City
Brooklyn......		April 30, May 1, 9, 10, 12, June 21, 22, 23, Sept. 14, 15	April 23, 24, 25, 26, June 14, 15, 16, Oct. 2, 3, 4	May 14, 15, 16, 17, July 17, 18, 19, Sept. 10, 11, 12	July 1, 3, 4, Aug. 10, 11, 12, Sept. 21, 22, 23	June 26, 27, 28, 30, Aug. 13, 14, 15, Sept. 18, 19, 20	July 6, 7, 8, Aug. 20, 21, 22, Sept. 28, 29, 30	July 12, 13, 14, 15, 17, Aug. 18, 19, Sept. 25, 26, 27
Athletic.......	April 27, 28, 29, May 13, July 21, 22, 24, Sept. 16, Oct. 11, 13		May 14, 15, 16, 17, June 9, 11, 12, Oct. 2, 6, 8, 9	May 2, 3, 4, 5, June 14, 15, 16, Oct. 2, 3, 4	July 6, 7, 8, 10, 17, 18, 19, 20, Sept. 18, 19, 20	July 12, 13, 14, 15, Aug. 20, 21, 22, Sept. 21, 22, 23	July 1, 3, 4, Aug. 10, 11, 12, Sept. 25, 26, 27	June 26, 27, 28, 30, Aug. 13, 14, 15, Sept. 28, 29, 30
Baltimore.....	May 2, 3, 5, 6, June 17, 19, 24, Oct. 14, 15, 16	April 18, 19, 20, 21, July 17, 18, 19, Sept. 10, 11, 12		May 9, 10, 11, 12, July 20, 21, 23, Sept. 13, 14, 15	July 12, 13, 14, 15, Aug. 17, 18, 19, Sept. 13, 19, 20	July 1, 3, 4, 4, Aug. 10, 11, 12, Sept. 25, 26, 27	July 12, 13, 14, 15, 17, Aug. 18, 19, Sept. 13, 19, 20	July 6, 7, 8, 10, Aug. 20, 21, 22, Sept. 21, 22, 23
Cleveland.....	April 18, 19, 21, 22, June 9, 10, 12, Oct. 6, 7, 9	April 23, 24, 25, June 13, 18, 19, 20, Oct. 15, 16, 17	April 27, 28, 30, May 1, June 21, 22, 23, Oct. 11, 12, 13		July 12, 13, 14, 15, Aug. 20, 21, 22, Sept. 25, 26, 27	July 6, 7, 8, 10, Aug. 17, 18, 19, Sept. 28, 29, 30	June 25, 27, 28, 30, Aug. 13, 14, 15, Sept. 21, 22, 23	July 1, 3, 4, 4, Aug. 10, 11, 12, Sept. 18, 19, 20

Cincinnati	May 30 June 1 July 29 31 Aug. 1 30 Sept. 1 2	June 4 5 6 7 July 26 27 28 Sept. 3 4 5	May 25 26 28 29 Aug. 6 7 8 25 27 28	May 19 21 22 23 Aug. 2 3 4 6 7 8			April 28 29 May 1 2 June 21 23 24 Oct. 2 3 4	April 23 24 25 26 June 16 17 19 Sept. 14 15 16	April 18 19 21 22 June 13 14 15 Sept. 11 12 13
Louisville	May 25 26 27 29 Aug. 6 7 8 Sept. 7 8 9	May 19 21 22 23 Aug. 2 3 4 25 27 28	May 30 June 1 2 July 30 31 Aug. 1 Sept. 1	June 4 5 6 7 July 26 27 28 Sept. 3 4 5	May 12 13 15 16 July 17 18 19 Oct. 5 6 7				April 18 19 21 22 June 13 14 15 Sept. 11 12 13	
St. Louis	June 3 5 6 7 Aug. 3 4 5 Sept. 3 4 5	May 30 June 1 2 Aug. 6 7 8 30 31 Sept. 1	May 19 21 22 23 July 26 27 28 Sept. 6 7 8	May 24 25 26 28 July 30 31 Aug. 25 27 28	May 8 9 10 11 June 9 10 11 Oct. 11 12 13 14			May 3 4 5 6 July 21 22 24 Oct. 9 10 11		
Kansas City	May 19 20 22 23 July 26 27 28 Aug. 25 26 28	May 25 26 28 29 July 30 31 Aug. 1 Sept. 6 7 8	June 4 5 6 7 Aug. 2 3 4 Sept. 3 4 5	May 30 June 1 2 6 7 8 Aug. 30 31 Sept. 1	May 3 4 5 6 July 21 22 24 Oct. 9 10 11				May 12 13 15 16 July 17 18 19 Oct. 5 6 7	

THE REPRESENTATIVE B. B. PAPER OF AMERICA.

THE SPORTING * LIFE.

Recognized by all Organizations, all Players, and the entire Base Ball loving public as the best Base Ball Journal published.

It chronicles all sporting events. Nothing escapes it, and it leads in news-gathering. It has the best corps of editors and correspondents ever organized, and contains more reading matter than any similar paper in the world.

Has a larger SWORN and PROVED circulation than any other sporting or base ball paper, or indeed any number of similar papers combined in the country, if not in the world.

The only sporting paper in America which has all the mechanical work performed under its own roof, and which is printed on its own Web Perfecting Press, with a capacity of 15,000 printed, cut and folded complete papers per hour.

To read it once is to swear by it forever.

PUBLISHED BY

SPORTING LIFE PUBLISHING CO.,

202 S. NINTH ST.,

P. O. Box 948.   Philadelphia, Pa.

F. C. RICHTER, Editor.

SUBSCRIPTION TERMS:
IN ADVANCE.

One year,	$2.25
Six months,	1.25
Three months,	.65
Single Copies,	.05

For sale by all Newsdealers in the United States and Canada.

Sample Copies Free. Send for one.

THE
New York Sporting Times

ILLUSTRATED.

Published Sunday Morning. Contains PORTRAITS of all the Prominent Ball Players.

The BEST SPORTING PAPER in America. For Sale at all NEWS STANDS. Price Five Cents. Subscription $2.00 per Year.

ADDRESS

THE SPORTING TIMES,

73 PARK ROW, NEW YORK.

THE
CHICAGO TRIBUNE.

The Western Sporting Authority.

THE SUNDAY EDITION OF THE CHICAGO TRIBUNE, and the Daily Edition throughout the playing season of 1888, will be found, as heretofore, indispensable to those who desire accurate, reliable, and comprehensive base ball records and reports.

Every club and club-room should keep THE SUNDAY TRIBUNE on file.

THE TURF DEPARTMENT

THE TRIBUNE is universally admitted to be without equal, and during 1888 it will be still further improved. Special telegraphic reports of the principal running and trotting meetings will be furnished, and particular attention be given to the performances of the American horses in England.

In other departments of sport THE TRIBUNE will maintain the superiority it has so long enjoyed.

TERMS:

SUNDAY EDITION, 24 Pages, per year, - $ 2.00
DAILY TRIBUNE, including Sunday, - - 10.00

Address,

THE TRIBUNE,
CHICAGO, ILL.

THE INTER OCEAN

Is published EVERY DAY IN THE YEAR, and holds the FIRST PLACE in public favor.

The **SPORTING NEWS** and **DRAMATIC DEPARTMENTS** of the INTER OCEAN are the ABLEST and MOST COMPLETE of any Paper in Chicago.

The SUNDAY INTER OCEAN is the BEST Literary Publication in America.

The Daily Inter Ocean, per Year, - - $8.00
The Sunday Inter Ocean, per Year, - - 2.00

Address,

THE INTER OCEAN,
CHICAGO.

CLIFTON HOUSE,

CHICAGO.

The Proprietors of the CLIFTON would respectfully solicit the patronage of the League and other traveling Base Ball Clubs, for the season of 1888. We offer a special rate of

$2.00 PER DAY,

And refer to all the League Clubs for the past five seasons, who have made their home with us, also to Messrs. A. G. SPALDING & BROS., 108 Madison St.

WOODCOCK & LORING,
PROPRIETORS.

SEASON OF 1888.

BASE BALL PRINTING!

Again Adopted by the NATIONAL LEAGUE and Other Principal Associations.

POSTERS
One Sheet, 28x42 inches.   Three Sheets, 28x42 inches each.

WINDOW HANGERS
In five colors.   Six striking designs.

ILLUMINATED SCORE CARDS
20 designs. Extra large Size.
All reduced in Price,

Send 25 cents in stamps for sample set of the Score Cards to

JOHN B. SAGE,
BUFFALO, N. Y.

THE MILWAUKEE, LAKE SHORE AND WESTERN RAILWAY.

THROUGH PALACE SLEEPING AND PARLOR CAR LINE
BETWEEN
CHICAGO and MILWAUKEE
APPLETON, WAUSAU, and ASHLAND, the GOGEBIC, PENO-KEE and MONTREAL IRON and MINERAL RANGES,
HURLEY, IRONWOOD, BESSEMER AND WAKEFIELD.
THE DIRECT LINE TO DULUTH.
And the Manufacturing Centers and Lumbering Districts of Central and Northern Wisconsin, Sheboygan, Manitowoc, Kaukauna, Appleton and Wausau. Special Inducements and Facilities offered for the location of Manufacturing establishments.

Close Connections at **ASHLAND AND DULUTH** for NORTHERN PACIFIC AND PACIFIC COAST POINTS.

TO SPORTSMEN. The most celebrated Fishing Resorts for Bass and Muskallonge in the Northwest are all reached by this Line—
GOGEBIC LAKE, THE EAGLE WATERS, PELICAN LAKE,
The Ontonagon, Brule and other Trout Streams.

Guide Books, Maps, Time Cards, and full information furnished on application to the Gen'l Passenger and Ticket Agent.

CHAS. L. RYDER, General Agent. } 105 Washington Street, CHICAGO.
ERNEST VLIET, City P. & T. Agt.   (114 Clark St. after May 1, 1888.)
H. F. WHITCOMB,   GEO. S. MARSH,
General Manager.   Gen'l P. & T. Agt.
MILWAUKEE, WIS.

FROM CHICAGO,
EAST AND SOUTH

TAKE THE

PENNSYLVANIA LINES,

Pittsburgh, Ft. Wayne & Chicago

RAILWAY,

(Fort Wayne Route.)

TO

PITTSBURGH, BALTIMORE, PHILADELPHIA, HARRISBURGH, WASHINGTON, NEW YORK, AND ALL EASTERN POINTS,

AND THE

Chicago, St. Louis & Pittsburgh R. R.

(Pan Handle Route,)

TO

COLUMBUS, CINCINNATI, INDIANAPOLIS, LOUISVILLE, AND ALL POINTS SOUTH,

AND

PITTSBURGH, AND ALL POINTS EAST.

JAS. McCREA, Gen'l Manager,   E. A. FORD, Gen'l Pass. Agt.,
PITTSBURGH, PA.
C. W. ADAMS, Ass't Gen. Pass. Agt., CHICAGO, ILL.

"VICTOR"

LIGHT ROADSTER SAFETY
TRICYCLE
JUNIOR BICYCLE

Comprise the Finest Line of "Cycles." They run easiest and wear longest.

SEND FOR COMPLETE DESCRIPTIVE CATALOGUE AND PRICE LIST.

A. G. SPALDING & BROS.

108 Madison St.,   241 Broadway,
CHICAGO.   NEW YORK.

THE YOUTH'S PREMIER

Is the Leading Boys' Bicycle.

BICYCLE SUNDRIES,
   BOYS' VELOCIPEDES,
     GIRLS' TRICYCLES,
       BICYCLE UNIFORMS.

Send for Catalogue.

TO BASE BALL PLAYERS.

Twelve years ago we issued a notice to Base Ball Players, announcing that we had engaged in the business of furnishing Base Ball Supplies, and soliciting their patronage. That our efforts to furnish satisfactory implements and paraphernalia have met with success, is evidenced by the remarkable increase in our business since that time. Having been for ten years prior to that date intimately identified with the game, we had acquired a practical knowledge of the wants of ball players; and it has always been our aim, instead of flooding the market with cheap, worthless goods that might please the trade but displease the player, to manufacture and sell articles of genuine merit only, and such as would give the most perfect satisfaction to players. With our practical experience in the game and being the largest manufacturers of everything that is necessary in the base ball player's outfit, we are now in position to anticipate the wants of players, and furnish a better grade of goods than any other house in the trade.

Manufacturers who have no reputation to sustain are continually offering inferior goods, which are readily sought after by the average dealers in base ball supplies, who, not being acquainted with the practical wants of players, are apt to regard only the low prices, and not the quality of the goods. It is our constant endeavor to manufacture only the very best goods, and to sell them at fair prices. Our well known trademark can be found on every article we manufacture in the base ball line, and is a guarantee of its quality.

As our business is largely by mail, we urge upon our patrons the importance of writing plainly the names of their town, county and State; and in order to save return express charges on money, to accompany their orders with draft, postoffice order, express money order, or currency for the amount due. In all cases where the goods are not satisfactory and exactly as represented by us, they may be returned, and the money will be refunded. We desire to sell all the goods we can, but we wish also to do more than this, and that is to please our customers in every instance. The established reputation of our goods, and the record we have made by the fair and liberal treatment of our customers, is the best guarantee that can be offered for the future.

With our two stores, in Chicago and New York, we are enabled to supply our customers more promptly than any other house in the trade. We carry duplicate and complete lines at both places, and our Eastern customers can order direct from our New York house, while the Western trade will be supplied from Chicago, or orders may be sent to any of our Depots of Supplies or Local Agencies, as may suit the convenience of the purchaser.

CHICAGO. **A. G. SPALDING & BROS,** NEW YORK.

UNIFORM DEPARTMENT.

OUR facilities for manufacturing Base Ball and all kinds of Athletic Clothing and Uniforms are the very best. These departments are under the supervision of experienced men, who are expert in designing and making Base Ball Uniforms. We would urge Clubs in their own interests not to make the mistake of intrusting their uniforms to local dealers, whose experience in this kind of work is necessarily limited, but profit by the experience and experiments of the leading professional clubs in the country, and send your orders direct to headquarters, and get a stylish and satisfactory outfit at a fair price.

Our Mr. J. W. Spalding has recently returned from Europe, where he selected a very large assortment of English flannels, which, with the special line of American flannels that are made exclusively for us, we are prepared to make Base Ball and Athletic Uniforms that cannot be equaled in America.

Self Measurement Blanks and Illustrated Price List of Uniforms furnished free upon application. Send 10c. to cover postage for Samples of Flannel and Belt Webbing, and receive a handsome engraved fashion plate, showing the different styles and prices. We can furnish complete Uniforms from $5.00 to $30.00 per man. It is impossible to give a complete price list in the "Guide," but will outline in a general way the average cost of complete Uniforms, mostly in use by Base Ball Clubs.

No. 0 Uniform, consisting of Shirt, Pants, Stockings, Cap, Belt and Necktie, without Shoes...each, $12 50
" 1 Uniform, same articles as above.......... " 10 00
" 2   "   "   "   "   " .... "   7 50
" 3   "   "   "   "   " .... "   5 00
" 4   "   "   "   "   " .... "   3 50

Extra for Padded Pants, from 75c. to $1.50 per pair.

Prices and full information for Self Measurement furnished upon application.

Correspondence from clubs and individuals solicited.

Special attention will be paid this season to the manufacture of cheap suits for Boys.

CHICAGO. A. G. SPALDING & BROS. NEW YORK.

COMPLETE UNIFORMS.

STYLE B.   STYLE C.   STYLE D.

BASE BALL UNIFORMS.

Our line of Flannels for Base Ball Uniforms consists of five qualities and over forty different patterns. Each grade is kept up to the highest point of excellence, and the patterns are changed every year. We will leave nothing undone to maintain our reputation in this department, and base ball players are assured that, no matter which grade of uniform is selected, it will be the very best that can be FURNISHED FOR THE MONEY.

NO. 0 UNIFORM.

NO. 0. BEST QUALITY LEAGUE OR ASSOCIATION CLUB UNIFORM. The flannel used in this uniform is manufactured exclusively for us, and which we have used for the past six years. For the durability of the material and superiority of the styles and workmanship, we refer to all clubs who have used our uniforms. We have made uniforms for the following leading clubs in

THE LEAGUE—NEW YORK, CHICAGO, BOSTON, DETROIT, WASHINGTON, INDIANAPOLIS, PITTSBURGH.

THE ASSOCIATION—ST. LOUIS, BROOKLYN, CINCINNATI, METROPOLITAN, LOUISVILLE, CLEVELAND.

And for the majority of the clubs of the N. E. League, International League, Southern League, Western League, N. W. League and others. We have fifteen different styles or colors as follows: No. 1, White; No. 2, Light Blue, mixed; No. 3, Stone Drab, mixed; No. 4, Brown, mixed; No. 5, Steel Gray; No. 6, White, narrow green stripe; No. 7, White, narrow blue stripe; No. 8, Gray, large blue check; No. 9, Light Drab; No. 10, White, blue and red cross bars; No. 11, Dark Brown; No. 12, Navy Blue; No. 13, Maroon; No. 14, Royal Blue; No. 15, Old Gold.

CHICAGO. A. G. SPALDING & BROS. NEW YORK.

BASE BALL UNIFORMS—Continued.

No. o.	Quality	Shirts, any style................................	Each,	$5	00
" o.	"	Pants, "	"	4	50
" o.	"	Stockings......................................	"	1	50
" o.	"	Caps...	"	1	00
" oo or o Belt ....,................................			"		50

Necktie to match trimmings.
Uniform complete w.thout Shoes............................ $12 50
Extra for Padded Pants................................Each pair, 1 50

NO. 1 UNIFORM.

NO. 1 UNIFORM. The flannel used in this uniform is the same quality as the No. o grade, but lighter in weight. We have fifteen styles and colors as follows: No. 16, White; No. 17, Yale Gray; No. 18, Drab, mixed; No. 19, Shaker Gray; No. 20, Steel, mixed; No. 21, Navy Blue; No. 22, Dark Brown; No. 23, Maroon; No. 24, Royal Blue; No. 25, Old Gold; No. 26, Scarlet; No. 27, Green; No. 28, Light Brown; No. 29, Dark Gray; No. 30, Light Gray.

PRICE.

No. 1.	Quality	Shirt, any style................................	Each,	$4	00
" 1.	"	Pants, "	"	3	75
" 1.	"	Stockings	"	1	00
" 1st	"	Caps...	"		75
" o or 2	"	Belt...	"		50

Necktie to match trimmings.
Uniform complete without shoes............................. $10 00
Extra for Padded Pants................................Each pair, 1 50

NO. 2 UNIFORM.

NO. 2 UNIFORM. Made of 4½ oz. twilled flannel in the following colors: No. 31, White; No. 32, Yale Gray; No. 33, Shaker Gray; No. 34, Steel, mixed; No. 35, Navy Blue.

PRICE.

No. 2.	Quality	Shirt, any style................................	Each,	$3	00
" 2.	"	Pants, "	"	2	75
" 2.	"	Stockings	"		75
" 2d	"	Caps...	"		60
" 1 or 3	"	Belt...	"		40

Necktie to match trimmings.
Uniform complete without Shoes............................ $7 50
Extra for Padded Pants................................Each pair, 1 50

NO. 3 UNIFORM.

NO. 3 UNIFORM. Made of three colors of flannel—White, Gray, Navy Blue. Heavy and strong. The best value at the price.

PRICE.

No. 3.	Quality	Shirt, any style................................	Each,	$2	00
" 3.	"	Pants, "	"	1	75
" 3.	"	Stockings	"		50
" 3.	"	Caps...	"		50
" 3 or 4	"	Belt...	"		25

Uniform complete without Shoes............................ $5 00
Extra for Padded Pants................................Each pair, 1 00

CHICAGO. **A. G. SPALDING & BROS.** NEW YORK.

BASE BALL UNIFORMS—Continued.
NO. 4 UNIFORM.

Made of a White Shaker Flannel and a Gray Cotton Cloth.

PRICE.

No. 4.	Quality Shirt, plain, pleat or lace	Each, $1 60
" 4.	" Pants	" 1 25
" 4.	" Stockings	" 25
Canton Flannel Cap, lined		" 25
No. 4 Belt		" 15

Uniform complete without Shoes $3 50
Extra for Padded Pants .... Each pair, 75

Special Measurement Blanks, Samples of Flannel and Belt Webbing for all of above Uniforms furnished upon application.

ATHLETIC CLOTHING.

Our facilities for manufacturing Base Ball, Cricket, Lawn Tennis, Boating, Bicycle and all other styles of Uniforms for Athletic and Sporting purposes, are unequaled.

In this Department we employ both at Chicago and New York a thoroughly practical and scientific cutter, one who is fully capable of making fine clothing for ordinary wear, but is especially educated in the cutting of Athletic Clothing. We would urge clubs not to make the mistake of intrusting the making of their uniforms to local dealers, whose experience in this kind of work is necessarily limited.

BASE BALL SHIRTS.

No. 0.	League Club Shirts, any style			Each,	$5 00
" 1.	First Quality "	"		"	4 00
" 2.	Second "	"	"	"	3 00
" 3.	Third "	"	"	"	2 00
" 4.	Fourth "	"	lace or button only	"	1 60

For description of Flannels used in making these Shirts, see Complete Uniforms.

TO MEASURE FOR SHIRT.

Size of collar worn, length of sleeve from shoulder seam to wrist with arm raised and bent, size around chest.

Send for our special measurement blank.

BASE BALL PANTS.

No. 0.	League Club Pants, any style			Each,	$4 50
" 1.	First Quality "	"	"	"	3 75
" 2.	Second "	"	"	"	2 75
" 3.	Third "	"	"	"	1 75
" 4.	Fourth "	"	"	"	1 25
					Each Pair.

For Padding and Quilting No. 0, 1 or 2 Quality at hips and knees.... $1 50
" " " " " 3 Quality at hips and knees........... 1 00
" " " " " 4 " " " 75

TO MEASURE FOR PANTS.

Outseam from waistband to 8 inches below knee. Inseam from crotch to 8 inches below knee, around waist, around hips.

Send for our special measurement blank.

CHICAGO. **A. G. SPALDING & BROS.** NEW YORK.

BASE BALL SHIRTS.

		EACH.
No. 0.	Extra quality shirt, of extra heavy flannel, made expressly for our League Club trade, any style, white, blue or gray...................................	$5 00
" 1.	First quality shirt, any style.................	4 00
" 2.	Second quality shirt, any style..............	3 00
" 3.	Third quality shirt, any style................	2 00
" 4.	Fourth quality shirt, lace or button only.	1 00

TO MEASURE FOR SHIRT.—Size Collar worn   Length of Sleeve from shoulder seam to wrist, with arm raised and bent.

BASE BALL PANTS.

		EACH.
No. 0.	Extra quality flannel pants..	$4 50
" 1.	First quality pants	3 75
" 2.	Second quality pants.......	2 75
" 3.	Third quality pants.........	1 75
" 4.	Fourth quality pants.......	1 25

For Padding and Quilting from hip to knee, each, 75c, $1 00 and $1 50.

TO MEASURE FOR PANTS.—Outseam from waistband to 8 inches below knee. Inseam from crotch to 8 inches below knee. Around waist. Around hips.

A COMPLETE PRICE LIST FURNISHED UPON APPLICATION.

<u>CHICAGO.</u> **A. G. SPALDING & BROS.** <u>NEW YORK.</u>

BASE BALL CAPS.

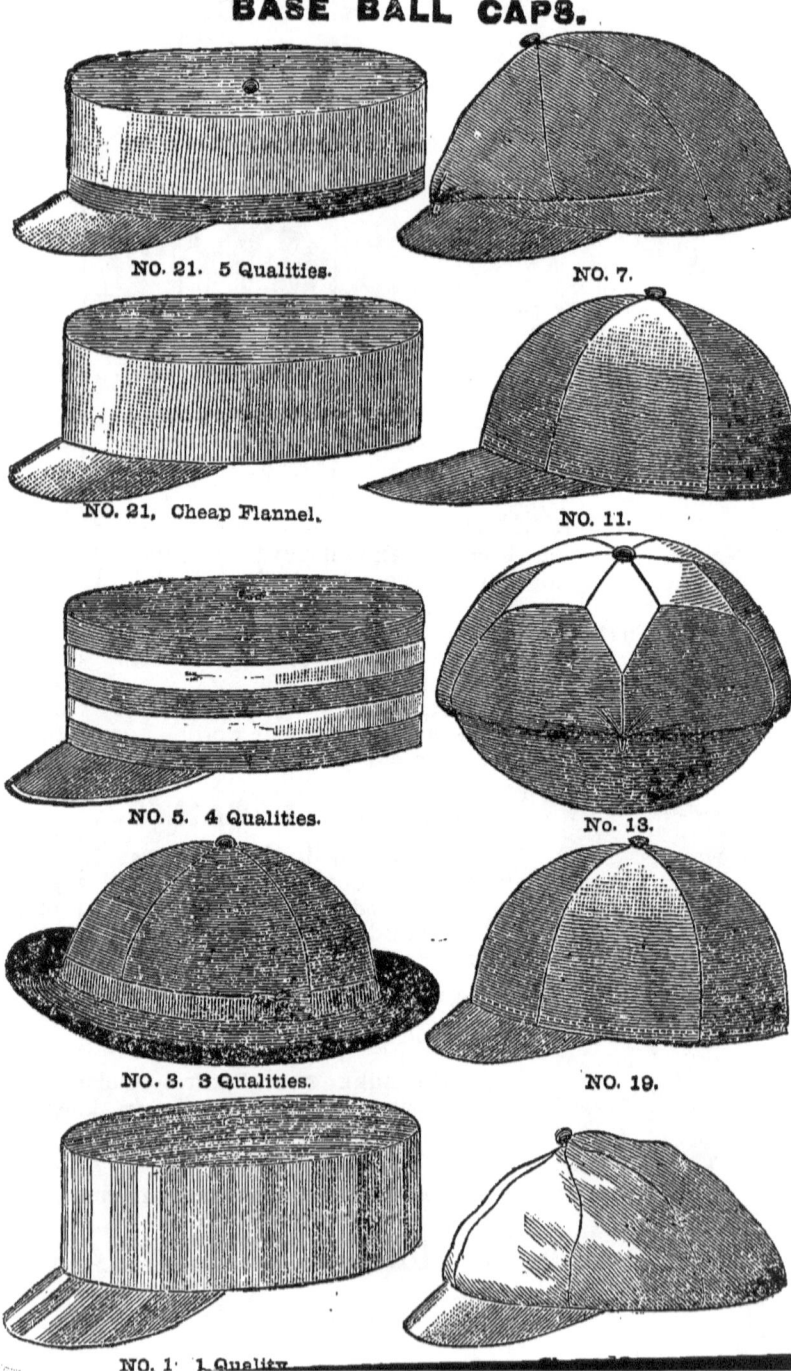

NO. 21. 5 Qualities.
NO. 7.
NO. 21. Cheap Flannel.
NO. 11.
NO. 5. 4 Qualities.
No. 13.
NO. 3. 3 Qualities.
NO. 19.
NO. 1. 1 Quality.

BASE BALL HATS AND CAPS.

Our line of Base Ball Hats and Caps is unequaled for quality, style, workmanship and variety. Please note carefully before ordering what styles and colors we furnish in each quality, so that there may be no delay in filling orders.

0 QUALITY—This quality we make in any style from the same flannel that we use in League Uniforms. Colors, white, red, royal blue, navy blue, brown, maroon, old gold and nine patterns of grays, stripes and checks, as shown on our No. 0 Sample Card of Uniforms.

1ST QUALITY—This quality we make in any style and of the following colors: White, red, royal blue, navy blue, brown, maroon, old gold, green, or any of the grays and mixes, as shown in our No. 1 Uniform Sample Card.

2D QUALITY—Any style. Colors, white, red, royal blue, navy blue, light gray, medium gray, dark gray.

3D QUALITY—Any style, except hats; same colors as 2d Quality.

4TH QUALITY—Any style, except hats, and No. 5 Chicago style; colors same as 2d and 3d qualities.

CHEAP FLANNEL CAPS—Made in Style 21 only; colors, white, red, or royal blue.

CHEAP MUSLIN CAPS—Style 19 only; color, white, red or royal blue.

NO. 1 STYLE CAP—We make this cap from a special imported striped flannel, of which we carry in stock the following patterns in ¾ and 1¼ inch stripes: Black and white, maroon and white, royal blue and white, blue and black, black and scarlet, black and orange.

		EACH.
NO. 3. B. B. HAT	0 Quality, (For colors see above)	$2 00
	1st " " " "	1 50
	2d " " " "	1 25
NO. 1. PARTI-COLORED CAPS—1st Quality		1 00
¾ and 1¼ inch Stripes.		
NO. 5. CHICAGO CAP... Plain or with Bands.	0 Quality, (For colors see above)	$1 00
	1st " " " "	75
	2d " " " "	65
	3d " " " "	50
NO. 7. BOSTON STYLE CAP	0 Quality, (For colors see above)	$1 00
	1st " " " "	75
	2d " " " "	65
	3d " " " "	50
	4th " " " "	40
NO. 11. JOCKEY SHAPE CAP	0 Quality, (For colors see above)	$1 00
	1st " " " "	75
	2d " " " "	65
	3d " " " "	50
	4th " " " "	40
NO. 13. BOSTON STYLE CAP, With Star	0 Quality, (For colors see above)	$1 00
	1st " " " "	75
	2d " " " "	65
	3d " " " "	50
	4th " " " "	40
NO. 19. SKULL CAP	0 Quality, (For colors see above)	$1 00
	1st " " " "	75
	2d " " " "	65
	3d " " " "	50
	4th " " " "	40
NO. 21. COLLEGE STYLE CAP	0 Quality, (For colors see above)	$1 00
	1st " " " "	75
	2d " " " "	65
	3d " " " "	50
	4th " " " "	40
CHEAP FLANNEL CAPS	Lined, (For colors see above)	$0 25
	Unlined, " " "	15
CHEAP MUSLIN CAPS, Unlined	Per doz.,	1 20

CHICAGO. A. G. SPALDING & BROS. NEW YORK.

SPALDING'S BASE BALL BELTS.

No. oo or League Belt.

No. o and 3 Style of Belt.

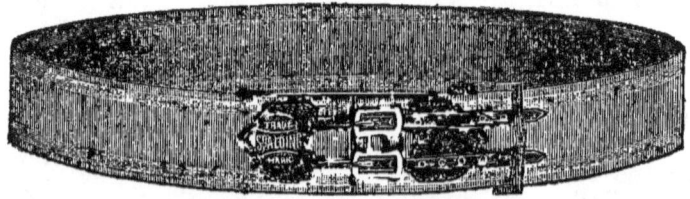

No. 1 and 2 Style of Belt.

Our Worsted Web Belts are made of the best webbing 2½ inches wide. We use the following colors:

A, Red; B, Blue; C. Navy Blue; D, Brown; E, Black; F, White; J, Maroon; G, Red, White Edge; H, Blue, White Edge; K, Old Gold.

No. oo.	League belt, large nickel-plated buckle............Each,	$0 50
" o,	Professional belt, nickel plated buckle............ "	50
" 1,	Belt, leather mounted, double strap, nickel buckle..... "	40
" 2,	Belt, leather m'nt'd, double strap, leather cov'd buckle, "	50

COTTON WEB BELT.

Our Cotton Web Belts are made of the best cotton webbing, 2½ inches wide, fast colors. We furnish the following colors:

L, Red; M, Blue; N, Red, White Edge; O, Blue, White Edge; P, Red, White and Blue; Q, White; R, Red and White Narrow Stripe; S, Blue and White Narrow Stripe; T, Maroon; V, Navy Blue.

No. 3.	Belt, large nickel buckle....................Each,	$0 30
" 4,	Belt, leather mounted, single strap and buckle..... "	20
" 5,	Belt, 2 inch web, single strap, white, blue or red, Boys' sizes only................................. "	10

Any of the above belts mailed postpaid on receipt of price.

CHICAGO. **A. G. SPALDING & BROS.** NEW YORK.

Spalding's Special Hand Made
KANGAROO BALL SHOE
FOR
Professional Players.

No. 2-0, - - - Price, $7.00.

WE now have on the third floor of our New York Store a thoroughly equipped Shoe Factory for the manufacture of fine Base Ball and Athletic Shoes. This department of our business is under the immediate charge and supervision of Wm. Dowling, who for several years past has enjoyed the reputation of being the leading maker of Athletic Shoes in New York. We employ in this department the most skilful workmen, and use only the very best material and are prepared to take special orders and make a special last for professional players.

The special attention of Ball players is called to our new genuine KANGAROO BASE BALL SHOE, which will be used this coming season by the Chicago, New York, Detroit, and other prominent League players.

The above cut represents this Shoe, which is made from selected genuine Kangaroo skin, all hand sewed, slipper heel, cut low in front, and wide, so they can be laced tight or loose as the player likes.

Each pair is provided with alligator laces, and the whole Shoe made with reference to comfort and the hard usage required of it.

Our new Hand Forged Shoe Plates—for toe and heel—will be riveted on when required, without additional expense.

HOW TO MEASURE.

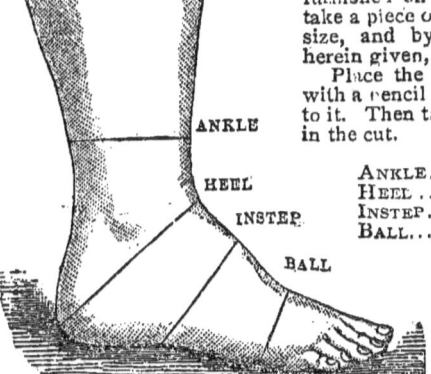

MEASUREMENT BLANKS will be furnished on application, or a player can take a piece of manila paper of sufficient size, and by following the directions herein given, can take his own measure:

Place the foot flat on the paper, and with a pencil draw around the foot close to it. Then take other measures as shown in the cut.

LEFT FOOT.

ANKLE	INCHES.
HEEL	"
INSTEP	"
BALL	"

Ball Players will bear in mind that we make a special last for each man, which will be kept for future use. Satisfaction both as to fit and quality of shoe guaranteed.

CHICAGO. A. G. SPALDING & BROS. NEW YORK.

Spalding's Trade-Marked Base Ball Shoes.

SPALDING'S SPECIAL LEAGUE SHOE.

No. 0.

Per Pair.

No. 0. Spalding's Special League Shoe. Used by League Players. Made of choicest selected Calf Skin, with natural side out, Hand Sewed and Warranted, superior to any Shoe on the market except our No. 2-0 Shoe... $6 00

CHICAGO CLUB SHOE.

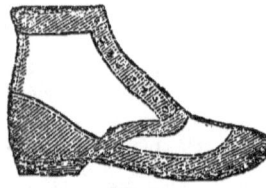

No. 2.

No. 2. Chicago Club Shoe, extra quality canvas, foxed with French calf. Made on best model lasts, and is in every way a fine shoe. The Standard Screw Fastener is used. Warranted... $4 00

AMATEUR, OR PRACTICE SHOE.

No. 3.

No. 3. Amateur, or Practice Shoe. Good quality, canvas strap over ball.... $2 00

AMATEUR BASE BALL SHOE FOR BOYS.

No. 3X. Amateur Base Ball Shoe, for boys. Second quality canvas............... $1 50

OXFORD TIE BASE BALL SHOE.

No. 4.

No. 4. Oxford Tie Base Ball Shoe, Low cut, canvas.. $2 00

CHICAGO. **A. G. SPALDING & BROS.** NEW YORK.

SPALDING'S SHOE PLATES.

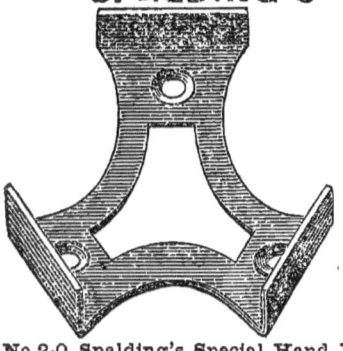

We have experienced more difficulty in the manufacture of a Shoe Plate than any other article that goes to make up a ball player's outfit, but at last we are prepared to offer something that will give the player satisfactory service.

Special attention is called to our new No. 2-0 Hand Forged English Steel Shoe Plate, made at our own factory.

The peculiar shape of this plate is shown in the adjoining cut. It is light, strong, and so tempered that it will not bend or break, and the League and Association players who have used it pronounce it perfect.

No. 2-0.	Spalding's Special Hand Forged English Steel Shoe Toe and Heel Plates, best made, put up in box with screws, per set of four plates	$0 75
No. 0.	Spalding's Tempered Steel Shoe Plate, made of imported steel, and warranted not to bend or break; put up with screws..Per Pair,	0 50
No. 1.	Professional Steel Shoe Plate, similar in shape and style to the No. 0 Plate, put up with screws.................Per Pair,	25
No. 2.	Amateur Steel Shoe Plate, put up with screws... "	15

PITCHER'S TOE PLATE.

Made of heavy brass, to be worn on the toe of the right shoe. A thorough protection to the shoe, and a valuable assistant in pitching. All professionals use them.

Each............50c.

Any of above plates sent postpaid on receipt of price.

SPALDING'S
BASE BALL STOCKINGS.

		PER DOZ.
No. 0.	League Regulation, made of the finest worsted yarn. The following colors can be obtained: White, Light Blue, Navy Blue, Scarlet, Gray, Green, Old Gold, Brown..	$18 00
No. 1.	Fine Quality Woolen Stockings, Scarlet, Blue or Brown...................	12 00
No. 2.	Good Quality Woolen Stockings, Scarlet, Blue or Brown................	9 00
No. 3.	Second Quality Woolen Stockings, Scarlet or Blue........................	6 00
No. 4.	Cotton..	3 50
No. 5.	"	2 50

Sample pair mailed on receipt of price.

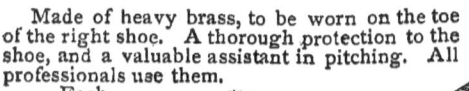

CHICAGO. A. G. SPALDING & BROS. NEW YORK.

Spalding's Trade-Marked Catchers' Mask.

The suit for infringement on Catchers' Masks brought against us by F. W. Thayer, of Boston, was after a two years' litigation decided against us in the U. S. District Court, and in settlement for back damages we arranged to protect all of our customers.

Ball players and dealers in Base Ball Goods are cautioned against buying any Catchers' Masks unless made under license from Thayer, and plainly stamped "Manufactured under Thayer's Patent."

At present it would be considered unsafe and even dangerous for a catcher to face the swift underhand throwing of the present day unless protected by a reliable mask. The increased demand for these goods has brought manufacturers into the field who, having no reputation to sustain, have vied with each other to see how *cheaply* they could make a so-called mask, and in consequence have ignored the essential qualification, *strength*. A cheaply made, inferior quality of mask is much worse than no protection at all, for a broken wire, or one that will not stand the force of the ball without caving in, is liable to disfigure a player for life. Our trade-marked masks are made of the very best hard wire, plated to prevent rusting, and well trimmed, and every one is a thorough face protector. We make them in four grades as described below.

Beware of counterfeits. *None genuine without our trade-mark stamped on each mask.*

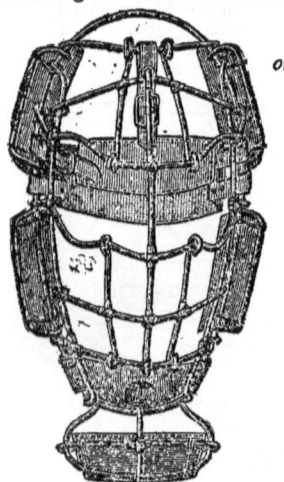

No. 3-0 Mask.

No. 2-0 Mask.

No. 3-0. Spalding's New Patented Neck-Protecting Mask. This mask has a peculiar shaped extension at the bottom which affords the same protection to the neck as the mask does to the face. It does not interfere in the slightest degree with the free movement of the head and is the only mask made which affords perfect protection to a catcher. The entire mask is constructed of the best hardened wire, extra heavy padded with goat hair, and the padding faced with the best imported dogskin, which is impervious to perspiration, and always soft and pliable, each, $4 00

No. 2-0. Spalding's Special League Mask, used by all leading professional catchers, extra heavy wire, well padded with goat hair, and the padding faced with the best imported dogskin, which is impervious to perspiration, and retains its pliability and softness 3 50

CHICAGO. **A. G. SPALDING & BROS.** NEW YORK.

SPALDING'S TRADE-MARKED CATCHER'S MASKS.—Continued.

No. 1-0. SPALDING'S REGULATION LEAGUE MASK, made of heavy wire, well-padded and faced with horsehide, warranted first-class in every respect...$3 00

No. 1. SPALDING'S BOYS' LEAGUE MASK, made of heavy wire, equally as heavy in proportion to size as the No. 2-0 mask. It is made to fit a boy's face and gives the same protection as the League Mask.. 2 50

AMATEUR MASKS.

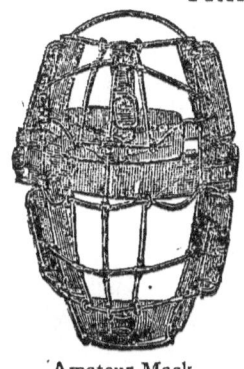

To meet the demand for good masks at a low price, we have manufactured a line of amateur masks, which are superior to any mask in the market at the same price. We do not guarantee these masks, and believe that our Trade-Marked Masks are worth more than the difference in price.

No. A. AMATEUR MASK, made the same size and general style as the League Mask, but with lighter wire and faced with leather (we guarantee this mask to be superior to so-called League or professional masks sold by other manufacturers)...................$1 75

No. B. BOYS' AMATEUR MASK, similar to No. A Mask, only made smaller to fit a boy's face...................... 1 50

Amateur Mask.

Any of the above masks mailed post-paid on receipt of price.

SPALDING'S TRADE-MARKED CATCHER'S GLOVES.

After considerable expense and many experiments we have finally perfected a Catcher's Glove that meets with general favor from professional catchers.

The old style of open backed gloves introduced by us several years ago is still adhered to, but the quality of material and workmanship has been materially improved, until now we are justified in claiming the best line of catcher's gloves in the market. These gloves do not interfere with throwing, can be easily put on and taken off, and no player subject to sore hands should be without a pair. Our new patent seamless palm glove is admittedly the finest glove ever made, and is used by all professional catchers. We make them in ten different grades, as follows:

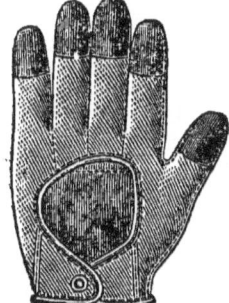

No. 4-0. SPALDING'S SPECIAL LEAGUE CATCHER'S GLOVE. Patented, full left hand. Made from choice soft buckskin, padded and lined with kid. Soft leather tips on fingers of left glove. This is the finest fielder's glove ever produced. Each pair packed in separate box.

Per pair............ $5 00

No. 4-0.

CHICAGO. A. G. SPALDING & BROS. NEW YORK.

SPALDING'S TRADE-MARKED CATCHER'S GLOVES.—Continued.

No. 3-0.

No. 30. Spalding's Special League Catcher's Gloves. Patented, both gloves without seams in palm. Full left-hand back stop glove, made of heaviest Indian-tanned buckskin, the very best that can be produced. The full left-hand glove is extra padded and sole leather finger tips to prevent the low curve balls from breaking or otherwise injuring the fingers. The right-hand glove is made with open back and fingerless, thoroughly padded. We especially recommend this glove for catchers. Each pair packed in separate box.................$5 00

No. 2-0. Spalding's League Regulation Catcher's Gloves. Patented, made of extra heavy Indian-tanned buck, and carefully selected with reference to the hard service required of them. This glove has full left-hand as shown in the illustration, with fingerless right hand, well padded, no seams in palm, and warranted. Each pair packed in separate box........................$3 50

No. 2-0.

No. 1-0. Spalding's League Catcher's Gloves, made of extra heavy Indian tanned buck, and carefully selected with special reference to the hard service required of them, open back, both hands fingerless, well padded, and fully warranted. We especially recommend this glove for catchers................. 2 50

No. 1. Spalding's Professional Gloves, made of Indian-tanned buckskin, open back, well padded, but not quite as heavy as the No. 0.. 2 00

AMATEUR CATCHER'S GLOVES.

Per pair.

No. A. Full Left Hand Catcher's Gloves, equal to most so-called League and professional gloves in the market..........$2 50
No. AA. Full Left Hand Glove, good quality................. 1 25
No. B. Spalding's Amateur Gloves, made of buckskin, open back, well padded and adapted for amateur players............ 1 50
No. C. Spalding's Practice Gloves, made of buckskin, open back, well padded..$1 00
No. D. Open back, a good glove at the price, made of light material, 75
No. E. Boys' size, cheap open back glove............. 50
No. F. Youths' size, cheap open back glove...................... 25

☞ Any of the above Gloves mailed postpaid on receipt of price. In ordering, please give size of ordinary dress glove usually worn.

CHICAGO. **A. G. SPALDING & BROS.** NEW YORK.

GRAY'S PATENT BODY PROTECTOR.

We now have the sole agency for this most useful device ever invented for the protection of catchers or umpires. This body protector renders it impossible for the catcher to be injured while playing close to the batter. It is made of best rubber and inflated with air, and is very light and pliable, and does not interfere in any way with the movements of the wearer, either in running, stooping or throwing. No catcher should be without one of these protectors. When not in use the air can be let out, and the protector rolled in a very small space.

No. 0. Extra heavy professional....$10 00
No. 1. Standard Amateur............ 6 00

CATCHERS' AND UMPIRE'S BREAST PROTECTOR.

This supplies a long felt want for the protection of Catchers and Umpires exposed to the swift underhand throwing. They are nicely made, well padded and quilted, and are used by nearly all professional Catchers and Umpires.

Chamois and Canvas..Each, $3 00.   Leather and Canvas, Each, ..$5 00

SPALDING'S PATENT CELLULOID UMPIRE INDICATOR.

As shown in the above cut is intended for the use of BASE BALL UMPIRES and SCORERS to keep tally of the number of Strikes and Balls that may be called. The illustration, which represents the exact size of the indicator gives a good idea of its construction and mode of handling. It can be easily operated by the thumb or finger while held in the palm of the hand. Now that the number of strikes has been increased it will be more difficult for the *umpire, scorer* and *spectator* to keep track of the balls and strikes called, and is therefore useful to all, spectator and scorer as well as umpire. It has been highly recommended by all League and Association umpires who have seen it.

Price, each 50c

By mail postpaid on receipt of price.

CHICAGO. **A. G. SPALDING & BROS.** NEW YORK.

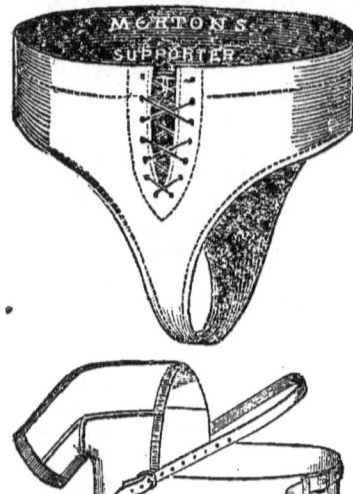

MORTON'S PERFECT SUPPORTER,

The best fitting, most comfortable and Effective Supporter yet devised. Used by ball players, athletes, boating men, and the theatrical and sporting profession generally. Made of best quality Canton flannel, with laced front, cool and pleasant to wear. Price. each 50 cts.

GUTH'S IMPROVED SUPPORTER.

Well known by Professional Ball Players. Price, Chamois Skin, $1.50. Muslin, 50 cents, Mailed on receipt of price.

ELASTIC AND SUSPENSORY BANDAGES.

Attention is called to the Elastic bandages on the accompanying cuts. The Shoulder Cap is used by most professional pitchers for preventing the dislocating of the shoulder, besides affording great relief to the arm, which becomes fatigued during the progress of the game. The Bandage at the elbow is for the support of the arm while throwing a ball, and is used extensively by ball players. The goods are woven of silk and cotton with elastic (and made to fit either right or left arm as the case may be), with light or strong pressure.

Shoulder Cap.

Arm Piece.   Elbow Piece.

DIRECTIONS FOR MEASUREMENT—For a Shoulder Cap.— Circumference around arm and chest separately. For an Elbow Piece.—Circumference below elbow, at elbow, above elbow. For an Arm Piece.—Circumference below elbow, and just above wrist.

	PRICES.	Silk.	Thread.
Shoulder Cap		$6 00	$4 50
Elbow Piece		2 50	1 75
Arm Piece		2 00	1 50

Suspensory Bandages, prices from 25 cents to $1.00, according to quality. Sent by mail on receipt of price.

MORTON'S PATENT SLIDING PAD.

A Necessity to Ball Players.

The Sliding Pad protects the side and hip of the player when undertaking to slide for a base.

Its use increases the player's confidence, and renders the act of sliding free from danger.

It is worn and recommended by all leading professional ball players.

No. 0.   Chamois lined, price each, by mail.................................$2 50
No. 1.   All canvas,   "   "   " 1 50

CHICAGO. A. G. SPALDING & BROS. NEW YORK.

BAT BAGS.

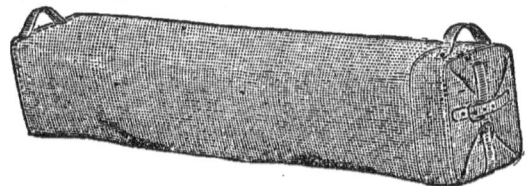

No. 0. **LEAGUE CLUB BAT BAG**, made of sole leather, name on side, to hold 1½ dozen bats.................................Each, $15 00

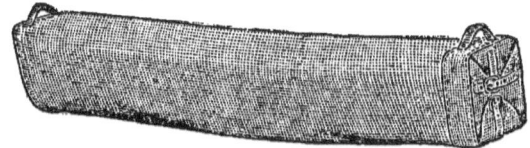

No. 1. **CANVAS BAT BAG**, heavy water proof canvas, leather ends, to hold 2 dozen bats.........................Each, $5 00

No. 2. **CANVAS BAT BAG**, heavy water proof canvas, leather end, to hold 1 dozen bats............................Each, $4 00

No. 01. **INDIVIDUAL LEATHER BAT BAG**, for 2 bats, Spalding's design, used by the players of the Chicago Club. Each, $4 00
No. 02. **INDIVIDUAL CANVAS BAT BAG**, heavy water-proof canvas, leather cap at both ends.......................Each, 1 50
No. 03. **INDIVIDUAL CANVAS BAT BAG**, heavy canvas, leather cap at one end..................................Each, 1 25

BASES.

No. 0. League Club Bases made of extra canvas, stuffed and quilted complete, with straps and spikes, without home plate...Per set of three, $7 50
No. 1. Canvas Bases, with straps and spikes, without home plate....... 5 00
No. 2. Cheap Canvas Bases, with straps and spikes, complete, without home plate........................... 4 00
Rubber Home Plate................each, 7 50
Marble Home Plate.. " 3 00
Iron Home Plate... " 1 00

CHICAGO. **A. G. SPALDING & BROS.** NEW YORK.

BRIGHT'S AUTOMATIC REGISTERING TURN STILE.

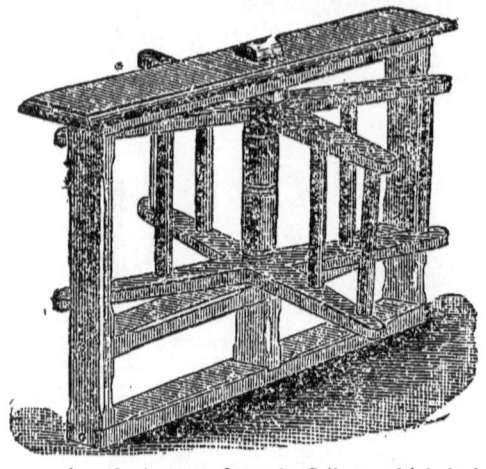

Is acknowledged to be the most reliable, durable and simple Turnstile made. It is designed especially for Base Ball and fair grounds, expositions, etc., and is an almost indispensable assistant in making a correct division of receipts and avoiding all possibility of the gate keeper's appropriating any portion of them, by accurately counting and registering each person passing through it. The movement registers from 1 to 10,000 and can easily and almost instantly be reversed to zero by any person having the key, without the necessity of removing from the Stile to which it is securely attached and locked. It is provided with all necessary stops, etc., to prevent its getting out of order through being handled by meddlesome persons, and is shipped complete and in readiness to be placed beside a doorway or other suitable entrance to inclosure, either permanent or temporary, and used without delay.

They are now in use by all League, American Association and minor league clubs throughout the United States, and their accuracy and reliability is shown by the fact that the receipts of each game are settled on the showing of the turnstile.

Orders from Base Ball Clubs should be sent in as early as possible, insuring their being filled before the beginning of the season.

Price, complete...$50 00

GRAND STAND CUSHIONS FOR BASE BALL GROUNDS.

The Chicago Club have for several seasons furnished cushions to their patrons at a nominal rental of 5 cents per game. It is a feature highly appreciated by base ball spectators. We are now manufacturing these cushions, and can supply them to clubs at 50 cents each. Special prices made when ordered in hundred lots.

CHICAGO. **A. G. SPALDING & BROS.** NEW YORK.

SPALDING'S SCORE BOOK.

Spalding's Pocket and Club Score Book continues to be the popular score book, and is used by all the leading scorers and base ball reporters. They are adapted for the spectator of ball games, who scores for his own amusement, as well as the official club scorer, who records the minutest detail. By this system, the art of scoring can be acquired in a single game.

Full instructions, with the latest League rules, accompany each book.

WHAT AUTHORITIES SAY OF IT:

Messrs. A. G. SPALDING & BROS.,

Gentlemen:—I have carefully examined the Spalding Score Book, and, without any hesitation, I cheerfully recommend it as the most complete system of scoring of which I have any knowledge.

Respectfully,

N. E. YOUNG, Official Scorer Nat'l League P. B. B. Clubs.

The score books issued by A. G. Spalding & Bros., of Chicago and New York, are the neatest thing of the kind we ever saw. Every lover of the game should have one. They are simple in their construction, and are easily understood.—*Cincinnati Enquirer.*

THE TRIBUNE has received from A. G. Spalding & Bros., a copy of their score book for use this year. The book or system is so far in advance of any other score book in the way of simplicity, convenience and accuracy, that it is not strange that it is in general use among scorers and reporters throughout the country.—*Chicago Tribune.*

A. G. Spalding & Bro.'s new score books will meet with unqualified indorsement of everybody who has ever undertaken to score a game of base ball. They are of various sizes, to meet the requirements both of the spectator who scores simply for his own satisfaction, and for official scores of clubs. The novel and commending feature of the book is the manner in which each of the squares opposite the name of the player is utilized by a division which originated with Mr. Spalding. Each of these squares is divided into five spaces by a diamond in its center, from the points of which lines extend to each of the four sides of the square. Each of these spaces is designed for the use of the scorer according to marks and signs given in the book. By thus dividing the squares into spaces he scores without the liability to make mistakes. The League rules of scoring are printed in the book.—*N. Y. Clipper.*

PRICES.

POCKET.   EACH.

No. 1. Paper Cover, 7 games...$ 10
No. 2. Board Cover, 22 games..   25
No. 3. Board Cover, 46 games..   50
Score Cards...   05
Reporter's Score Book, pocket size, leather bound........................... 1 00

CLUB BOOKS.

No. 4. Large Size, 30 games.. $1 00
No. 5.   "   "   60 games.. 1 75
No. 6.   "   "   90 games.. 2 50
No. 7.   "   "   120 games.. 3 00

Mailed upon receipt of price.

CHICAGO. A. G. SPALDING & BROS. NEW YORK.

THE REVISED EDITIONS OF
Spalding's Hand Books
For 1888. Price, 25c.

NUMBER THREE will be the revised book on

THE ART OF PITCHING AND FIELDING,

A work containing instructive chapters on all the latest points of play in base ball pitching, including special methods of delivery, the philosophy of the curve, the tactics of a strategist, headwork in pitching, the effects of speed, throwing to bases; and the revised book on The Art of Fielding, containing special articles on battery work in fielding, the pitcher and catcher as fielders, the infield, first base play, the second baseman's work, third base play, short fielding, the outsider's work, backing up, throwing to first base, the captain of a nine, how to captain a team, together with the best pitching and fielding records of the National League, American Association, and other professional organizations; mailed upon receipt of price, 25 cents.

NUMBER FOUR of the revised works for 1888, comprising the

ART OF BATTING AND BASE RUNNING,

Containing special chapters on scientific batting, placing the ball, sacrifice hitting, waiting for balls, the baseman's position, standing in good form, fungo batting, home run hitting, base hits, earned runs, etc., and the Art of Base Running, containing points of play in running bases, the rules for base running, etc., together with the leading batting averages in all the National Associations. Mailed on receipt of price, 25 cents.

What Competent Authorities Say of these Hand Books:

Walter C. Camp, the athletic instructor and noted ball player of Yale College says: I have looked over your works on "Pitching," "Batting," "Fielding," etc., published in Spalding's Library of Athletic Sports, and I am sure from the remembrance of my own experience, that they will be of inestimable value to lovers of sports; particularly your book on "Pitching," which I consider as thorough and satisfactory an explanation of the various curves as any I have read. The whole series will be of service to our younger players, especially of our colleges, and interesting to the older players.

The veteran, Harry Wright, says: For years I have read your books on the game of base ball and I have always found them both instructive and interesting. Your latest works on "The Art of Pitching," "Batting," "Fielding," etc., should be in the hands of all base ball players desiring to perfect themselves in the knowledge of the game. The scientific points of play, so clearly explained, should be carefully studied, and practice will eventually demonstrate their truthfulness. To quote, I will add: "Whatever may be said about luck, it is skill that leads to fortune."

That skillful and experienced strategist in pitching, T. S. Keefe, of the League team of New York, says: I have given your books on "Pitching," "Batting," and "Fielding," etc., a close perusal in every particular, and I can safely say that there is no work in the market so complete in all its details as your book on "The Art of Pitching." You have taken the game from its past low standing and placed it before the public in a manner that has greatly aided it in reaching its present high position among the sports of the day. The books on "Batting" and "Fielding," as well as on "Pitching," are not only valuable to the beginner, but they offer a great deal of food for reflection for the expert class of players. In fact, you have dealt with the game, in all its details in such a manner that every person can readily comprehend the full meaning of the points laid down in each book. Were the advice you offered followed by the professional class of players, it would have a great tendency to advance the game as far as science can command.

John M. Ward, the Captain of the New York League team, says: I have carefully read your book on "The Art of Pitching." You have treated the subject with an understanding possible only to one of your extended experience. I take pleasure in recommending the book as a most complete work on instructions in pitching.

CHICAGO. **A. G. SPALDING & BROS.** NEW YORK.

THE BOSS JUVENILE 5c. BALL.

Put up in a separate box and sealed as shown in following cut.

NO. 10. SPALDING'S BOSS BALL. Size 7½ inches; weight 3 oz. The best juvenile, two piece cover, five cent ball on the market. Each ball is put up in separate box and sealed with white band showing the Spalding trade-mark........................... Each, 5c. To Clubs. Per Doz. 50c.

If you cannot obtain this ball from your local dealer, send us 5 cents and we will mail you one.

CHICAGO. A. G. SPALDING & BROS. NEW YORK.

THE RATTLER JUVENILE 10c. BALL

Put up in separate box and sealed as shown in following cut.

NO. 9. **SPALDING'S RATTLER BALL**, White. Size 8⅝ inches; weight 4½ oz. The best and largest ten-cent ball made. Each ball is put up in a separate box and sealed with "white" band showing the Spalding trade-mark.................................... Each. 10c. To Clubs, Per Doz. $1 00

NO. 9B. **SPALDING'S BOYS' DEAD.** A good dead ball for boys. Put up in separate box and sealed.... 10c. 1 00

If you cannot obtain these ball from your local dealer, send ten cents to us and we will mail you one.

CHICAGO. A. G. SPALDING & BROS. NEW YORK.

Full Regulation Size.
20 CENT BALL.

Put up in a separate box and sealed as shown in following cut.

NO. 8. SPALDING'S EUREKA BALL, WHITE. Regulation size and weight. The best cheap ball for the money on the market. Each ball is put up in a separate box and sealed with white band, showing the Spalding trade-mark..........Each, 20c.

To Clubs, Per Doz. $2 00

If you cannot obtain this ball from your local dealer, send 20 cents to us and we will mail you one.

CHICAGO. **A. G. SPALDING & BROS.** NEW YORK.

www.ingramcontent.com/pod-product-compliance
Lightning Source LLC
Chambersburg PA
CBHW030249170426
43202CB00009B/686